40.—

Islamic Futures and Policy Studies

Series editor   *Ziauddin Sardar*

Business and Accounting Ethics in Islam

Trevor Gambling

and

Rifaat Ahmed Abdel Karim

MANSELL

LONDON AND NEW YORK

Learning Resources
Centre

First published in 1991 by
Mansell Publishing Limited, *A Cassell Imprint*
Villiers House, 41/47 Strand, London WC2N 5JE, England
387 Park Avenue South, New York, NY 10016–8810, USA

Reprinted 1993.

British Library Cataloguing in Publication Data

Gambling, Trevor
  Business and accounting ethics in Islam.
  1. Business enterprise. Ethical aspects. Islamic
  viewpoints
  I. Title   II. Karim, Rifaat Ahmed Abdel   III. Series
  297.5

  ISBN 0–7201–2074–8

Library of Congress Cataloging-in-Publication Data

Gambling, Trevor.
   Business and accounting ethics in Islam / Trevor Gambling and
Rifaat Ahmed Abdel Karim.
       p.   cm.—(Islamic futures and policy studies)
   Includes bibliographical references and index.
   ISBN 0–7201–2074–8
   1. Accounting—Islamic countries.   2. Accountants—Professional
ethics—Islamic countries.   3. Economics—Religious aspects—Islam.
4. Business ethics—Islamic countries.   5. Islamic ethics.
I. Abdel Karim, Rifaat Ahmed.   II. Title.   III. Series.
HF5616.I74G36   1991
174'.9657'0917671—dc20
                                                        90–13366
                                                        CIP

Printed and bound in Great Britain by
Ipswich Book Co. Ltd., Ipswich, Suffolk

21.6.96

Contents

v

Introduction

This is a book about present-day business and accounting, both in theory and practice. Its intended readership is primarily business-people and accountants, both Muslim and non-Muslim. It assumes a certain knowledge of accounting and business, but there is no assumption that the reader has any previous acquaintance with Islam.

The book is not 'religious' at all! Probably the most difficult thing for a non-Muslim to understand about Islam is that Muslims themselves do not see it as 'a religion'. According to their light, God created men and women to live in accordance with His Law. The Arabic word 'Islam' *means* 'obedience', so to be a Muslim is simply to be a fully developed human being. Human beings who are not Muslims by practice either do not know what God's laws are, or are perverting their natural instinct to obey them. For the Muslim, there can be no conflict between conscience and the Law:

> What does not exist for Muslims is conscience as an autonomous authority, because conscience can only appeal to God, or be touched by Him. But God is also the originator of those laws one would refuse to obey for reasons of conscience. Muslims follow not their consciences, but the Will of God. (Küng, 1987, p. 46)

Although it is essential to approach Islam in the way Muslims approach it if one is to say much of value about 'business and accounting ethics in Islam', this book is not a polemic on behalf of Islam. Nor is it a concealed plea for ecumenism. The arguments in these pages are founded upon a single fact: Muslims are people whose entire lives are spent in obedience (or disobedience) to an all-embracing and detailed code of law. The further fact

1

that they claim divine revelation for that code is not central to what we have to say. However, it does mean that these are laws for which there is no repeal, and from which there is no appeal.

History provides other examples of societies with unchanging laws, but these have been societies which permitted no social or economic change. We shall discuss the problems encountered by one such society, but a secondary significance of Islam for our purpose is that its laws actually support changes of this sort. Our objective is to say something about the function of accounting in *any* changing society.

The pragmatic nature of our approach means that we will bypass a number of issues which some readers might expect to find in a book with this title. For example, we will not be undertaking any substantial comparative study of the impact of religion on accounting under the Islamic and Judæo-Christian traditions. Primarily this is because there has been no direct input from any religious doctrine into Western business and accounting practice for many years. Also, the comparative approach tends to look for parallel and divergent developments from common sources. Muslims are unconcerned with possible Nestorian and Sabæan influences on Mohammed's personal thought-patterns; the Qur'an and the Sunnah are revealed truth, and independent of the Prophet's own world-view.

In the same way, we will not consider Islam as a cultural influence on accounting thought and practice. Islam is as universal in practice as it is in history. It seems unlikely that a single Islamic culture exists, any more than is the case with Christianity. An Arab culture may exist, and would certainly be influenced by Islam, but it differs greatly from the cultures to be found in Iran, or Indonesia, or Pakistan. A common legal code which permits and even encourages social change is not likely to produce a common culture. This must be especially so, when the communities which adopt it do not start from a common cultural base.

Abraham Briloff has suggested that the resources devoted in the West to the production of accounting principles would have been better spent on producing accountants *with* principles. Whatever the reader may think of the claims of Islam, it is the authors' hope that he or she will be inspired by our own belief that an amoral accounting code is neither essential nor desirable—and is, in fact, strictly impossible.

Bibliography

Küng, Hans, *Christianity and the World Religions* (London: Collins, 1987).

Chapter 1

Accounting, Religion and Society

The Law and Social Representation

At one level of thinking, a Muslim's approach to accounting is clear, as is his or her approach to everything else. God has given Man a Law to live by. This Law has been revealed to us at various times, in forms which were appropriate to the time and place. Starting with Adam and Eve, through Abraham, Moses and Jesus, the form of the Law has kept pace with Man's physical, psychological and social evolution. For Muslims, this evolution was completed in about the seventh century of the Christian Era, when the final form of the Law was revealed to Mohammed, who thereby became 'the Seal of the Prophets'. In its final form, this Law actually enjoins us to trade and make money, as we shall discuss in Chapter 2. As for accounting, the Qur'an directs traders to keep proper records of indebtedness. Apart from that, the general prohibitions on both waste and avarice, and unfair trading practices, imply a need for records which demonstrate what a business person has done. Finally, the Law enjoins the payment of a religious tax (*zakah*), which is assessed, in part, on wealth and trading profits.

A non-Muslim, even an atheist, might come to a similar position by other means. Trade, money—and income-based taxation—are obvious features of the human condition. There is a need to be able to demonstrate what has been going on, and in particular to be able to arrive at a definite figure of net income for a given entity over a given period of time. However, for non-Muslims and Muslims alike, there is a difficulty here: net income for a given period of time is not a natural phenomenon which can be measured objectively. In fact, it is a 'social representation', an abstract concept of the human mind, which can only be calculated by the use of arbitrary conventions (Thomas, 1969).

Again, these conventions can be found, although not in Nature itself. The

3

non-Muslim can discover them by observing existing business practice, or by taking thought from some first principles. Chapter 5 contains a critique of these approaches to accounting theory. For the Muslim, God's Law as revealed to the Prophet must specify an appropriate 'accounting theory', as it specifies everything else which men and women ought to do. We shall see, in Chapter 2, that the Qur'an does not lay down the details of the Law, but only its general principles. There are good reasons why this is so, but it requires Muslims to give a great deal of thought as to what those principles indicate they should do in particular. Chapter 7 of this book is an attempt to gather together these indications with respect to financial management and accounting into the basis for a coherent theory.

One might wonder why this Islamic theory was not already in place. For reasons which are discussed in the Appendix to Chapter 2, large-scale business and finance has come to the Muslim world as an importation. As a result, little if anything has been written about a specifically Islamic accounting theory. Moreover, non-Muslim experience with constructing such theories suggests that it may be a rather difficult task. If both Muslims and non-Muslims are sensible people who are attempting to maximize their 'incomes', the transcendentally correct measurement of income would be that which is maximized by what they can be seen to do. Chapter 4 will reveal the heart of the problem: it seems impossible to produce incontrovertible empirical support for any one theory!

Muslims would suppose that a correct application of the principles of Islamic Law must be able to resolve such a problem once and for all. On the other hand, while God may be disposed to suspend the apparent laws of Nature to produce miracles, it seems less likely, even to a believer, that He would do much to bring about the verification of a purely humanistic mental concept, or social representation. This would be especially so if the concept happens to be some way removed from the known and observable realities of Man's situation in the Universe. If God's Law had been revealed in detail, the issue would be of no consequence for Muslims. They could obey the Law in the confidence that any conflict between the Law and human rationality could only proceed from the fallibility of the latter.

But since Muslims have to apply human reasoning in order to arrive at the detail from basic principles, and given the long-standing inability of humanistic thinkers to solve the problem, we feel it is essential to adopt a more fundamental approach. Such outwardly 'real' phenomena as trade, administration, money, and the pursuit of surpluses may be no more than anthropocentric labels for what we can perceive of the workings of human societies. The Qur'an uses these labels so that anyone of normal intelligence

4

can understand the principles of the Law. However, their detailed application has to take account of what is known about the physical nature of the Universe.

A Societal Approach to Accounting Theory

It seems useful to start our analysis with a consideration of the place of human social organization in what is known of the natural science of the Universe. Some years ago, one of the co-authors suggested that accounting theory was part of personality, and so part of the collective culture (Gambling, 1974). This idea has become accepted, at least among those who find it difficult to agree that a 'positive economic theory' can underpin an equally positive accounting theory, applicable to all cultures, for all time. A culture is the collective version of the individual's personality, or world-view (*Weltanschauung*). It is a taxonomy by which one analyses what one perceives, and a box of tools for evaluating the result. Ideas about the supernatural and 'the unseen' are part of this taxonomy, on equal footing with ideas about self, other people, animals and the like. We seem just as well equipped to form ideas about unseen abstractions as about natural phenomena which we can experience directly.

However, culture (and hence accounting theory) is not a necessary feature of social organizations. Many animals have social organizations, but they have no culture. This is because animals are not strictly conscious, in the sense of being able to see themselves as something apart from the environment which surrounds them. A baboon behaves like a member of a troop of baboons because it cannot behave otherwise, and not because it thinks it right to do so. It has no consciousness of its own baboonery, no consciousness of its separation from other baboons, no consciousness of the separation of baboons from the rest of the Universe.

Man has emerged from the same condition. Australian Aboriginal culture speaks of a 'dreamtime' before creation was broken up, when human features and natural features were one and the same (Ròheim, 1947). The idea also occurs in the Judæo-Christian account of the Creation, with the first humans at one with Nature 'in a garden'. Islam adopts the same story of the Creation. Man, says the author of Genesis, became modern man when he broke away from this unity with Nature—'knowing good and evil' (3:5). 'Good' means 'what I want more of', so *Homo sapiens* became acquisitive, in the sense of going beyond gathering or creating what is necessary for subsistence, to creating surpluses.

5

The Limited Scope of Human Rationality

Why has Man developed civilization indirectly, through the neurotic pursuit of an ill-defined 'good'? Why cannot we decide what we need to do in some more direct fashion? It is because, while we have the facility of 'knowing good and evil', our conscious minds do not have the capacity to 'see things as they really are'? The proposition that human rationality can provide only a limited vision of reality is of considerable antiquity. The Old Testament expresses the idea in this way:

> For my thoughts are not your thoughts, neither are your ways my ways, saith the Lord.
> For as the heavens are higher than the earth, so are my ways higher than your ways, and my thoughts higher than your thoughts. (Isaiah 55:8–9)

A commentator on Sura 1:5 of the Qur'an, which reads: 'Praise be to God, the Cherisher and Sustainer of the Worlds', explains the unexpected use of the plural in the terms of Sufi mysticism:

> There are many worlds. . . . The mystical division between (1) *Nâsût*, the human world knowable by the senses, (2) *Malakût*, the invisible world of the angels, and (3) *Lâhût*, the divine world of reality, requires a whole volume to explain it. (Ali, 1968, p. 14; footnote 20)

Human rationality can only perceive a three-dimensional Universe in Cartesian space, and Newtonian physics explains the nature of physical phenomena in those terms. Neoclassical economics (and the other social sciences) provide models of social phenomena within the same limitations.

Modern physics and cosmology tell us that the Universe does not conform precisely to those principles. The problem with quantum physics is not that we do not have instruments of sufficient power or accuracy to measure subatomic phenomena, but that we, as human beings, cannot perceive them directly at all (Capra, 1975). The weak form of the anthropic cosmological principle suggests that we cannot perceive a Universe other than one which can support life (Barrow and Tipler, 1986). It may be that our world-view is even more restricted: we cannot perceive a Universe whose workings we cannot understand (Gambling, 1984). It follows that conscious human rationality cannot be addressing the total reality of the problems which face us.

This apparent restriction on human perception is probably a necessary part of the machinery for developing a 'civilization'. The reality is that the

Universe is a totally complex place where everything is a dependent variable of everything else. If we *were* conscious of this, we simply 'could not see the wood for the trees'. We would be unable to alter anything of our own free will; like the beasts of the field, we would have to obey our instincts.

A German writer, Arnold Gehlen, whose relevant work has not been translated into English, has supplied an ingenious explanation of how we overcome this problem. While animals are instinctively at one with their environment, *Homo sapiens* suffers from instinct reduction. This hiatus is filled by our consciousness, and it is this which enables us (or rather impels us) to pursue surpluses of goods, rather than subsistence. Our 'tunnel vision' of the Universe prevents us from seeing the weaker interactions in the reality which surrounds us. As a result, we can use comparatively simple-minded optimizing strategies to an apparent, and often real, advantage. The scientist's use of 'models' is a conscious extension of his or her natural instinct reduction. We shall see that *Homo sapiens* can build these models both as an individual and in a group; a group which shares such a model is a rather advanced type of social organization. Whether it operates within the individual or in the group, '[c]onsciousness is directed toward the structuring of human behavior' (Peter and Petryszak, 1980, p. 64, where Gehlen's work is discussed at length).

The essential irrationality of rational ideas poses problems for any theory of knowledge. The model of human thought employed in studies of 'artificial intelligence' is metaphysical: a construct built by the human consciousness itself, from first principles taken on faith. It cannot be derived through either neurology or psychology. Recent interest in developing electronic 'expert systems' has demonstrated the limitation of this model; the systems seem incapable of producing totally reliable judgement, even within what seem quite pedestrian areas of human expertise. 'Knowledge engineering' seems unable to capture the vital spark which makes human expertise live (Arnold *et al.*, 1985; Gambling, 1985). Colloquially, we call the unknown element in the system—'common sense'.

Common sense is nothing other than the unconscious sensibilities supplied by our central nervous system. It is quite independent of conscious rational thought. If consciousness structures human behaviour, as Gehlen suggests, common sense could be said to 'deconstruct' it. It is the mechanism by which *Homo sapiens* is able to bring the total interactivity of the real Universe back into (unconscious) consideration. Some part of common sense can be described as 'naive physics', and 'naive psychology'. An instinctive awareness that something can be pulled, but not pushed, by a piece of string, because it is 'pliable'; that people become uncooperative if thwarted, because 'their feelings are hurt'. Computers find it hard to handle these concepts, because they do not have muscles, nerves, etc.:

> [M]uch of the richness of texture of our introspective world comes, I think, from our knowledge of what it feels like when we do things like pushing, pulling, lifting; from, ultimately, proprioceptive sensors in our body-joints and muscles. I am not optimistic that we can capture this richness in a formalization in the foreseeable future. (Hayes, 1979, p. 254)

Dreyfus and Dreyfus (1986) refer to these deficiencies, and also draw attention to the apparently holistic nature of human expertise. Human intelligence is simply 'there', and does not seem to involve rational processes comparable to accessing a data-bank.

Animals use the same physical mechanisms of common sense as their sole method of perceiving their environment. Human intelligence is of a different order, and further analysis is needed to explain the operations of instinctive perception in civilized societies. Common sense could be said to exist at three levels of sophistication. The lowest level is pure instinct, which we share with the rest of the animal kingdom. This is largely epigenetic, or inborn; we remove our hands from heated surfaces, and (in general) feel considerable reluctance to mate with our nearer blood-relatives.

The second level is that of technical expertise: cabinet-making, surgery, playing chess. Of course, some animals also make use of tools, as when thrushes use a stone to break open a snail-shell, or some finches use thorns to pick grubs out of tree-bark. This type of common sense is purely instinctive, whether exhibited by animals or humans. Thus grand master chess-players have been shown to be able to recall in excess of 50,000 board settings (Chase and Simon, 1973). However, they do not achieve this by running through a list of past games until they find a match. Their knowledge of chess is holistic, in greater or lesser detail, and they react to it instinctively. This may be true of much of human activity (Eich, 1982). *Once the game or operation has started*, one might say of all human experts, as of the thrushes and finches, that they play or operate in a particular way, because they cannot do otherwise.

It follows that while people can be given formal instruction in chess, or any other technical matter, they are at best beginners so long as they have to rely upon conscious recollection of what they have been taught (Dreyfus and Dreyfus, 1986). Expertise comes with experience, and this is made up of the sights, sounds, smells and touch of chess pieces, instruments, tools, tissue, wood, and so on, collected by the central nervous system, rather than material which has been consciously 'learned'. When knowledge engineers interrogate an expert about his or her expertise, they are demanding that the expert actually create, for the first time, conscious, fragmented, rational statements about something which is largely a matter of instinct.

Nevertheless, there is a distinction between human experts and tool-using animals. Thrushes and finches use tools after a given technique because they have been conditioned to do so by some external force. They can never act otherwise, except under further, externally applied conditioning. There is no distinction between this sort of behaviour and the other instinctive behaviour classified under Level I common sense. By contrast, *Homo sapiens* has the facility to switch between unconscious reaction of this type and conscious model-building activity. This is the essential difference between the first and second levels of common sense. We can modify our own expertise by taking thought, combining the new insight with our original unconscious common sense—and acting upon it. If the new idea 'works', we are positively conditioned to repeat it unconsciously in the future.

Model-building is also subject to common sense. If this were not so, the initial application of a new insight would be hazardous. This third level of common sense operates through human social organization. Some aspects of human society replicate those of the animal kingdom, as in a family, or even in the 'firm' made up of a human expert and his or her assistants. However, a major function of human organizations is to overcome what we perceive as uncertainties and imperfections in our environments (Cleverley, 1973). This activity involves 'administration' and 'trading', and this is where our faculty for building abstract models of reality *as a group* comes into play. There is a difficulty here. We can 'see' our personal models 'inside our heads', but a group model must have some other method of making its form known to us in a collective fashion. We also need a collective method of assessing the relative 'goodness' of the various alternative courses of action before us.

How this is done, seems to form the third level of common sense, which is found in *Homo sapiens* alone. The lower levels both operate through the physical senses of touch, hearing, taste, smell and sight. It may be an original insight in this area, that human social organizations exist to communicate both the construction of models and their necessary, deconstructing common sense *collectively*, through shared experiences of exactly the same physical sensations. It is well known that human organizations operate through ritual activity (Cleverley, 1973; March and Olsen, 1980). These secular rituals do not differ from more overtly religious ones. They produce secular 'sacraments', which are 'outward and visible signs' of otherwise indescribable concepts (Gambling, 1987). Through them, we are able to *feel* things like 'wealth', 'civic order', 'shareholding' and so on. Accounting and finance are central to most of these rituals.

The Ritual Nature of Money

Ideas about value, and hence money and accounting, are the driving force behind civilization. They provide the benchmarks for optimizing the models of reality created by instinct reduction in Man. Although these phenomena are nowadays rationalized through economic theory, they antedate that theory, and even trade itself, by millennia. Their origin was in ritual activity, and this chapter argues that their ritual purpose is unchanged. The remaining chapters of this book will be arguing that economic theory is one of a number of basically similar, and (at the very least) equally likely explanations of the phenomenon it describes. This is because human consciousness, and humanistic logic, cannot grasp the nature of what it is that *Homo sapiens* is driven to pursue through the models we create, otherwise than as a parable.

The outcome of our activity is surpluses of value; because they are surplus to our subsistence needs, they are not consumed; because they represent the ultimate in 'goodness', they are sacred. From the earliest times, Man has felt the need to dedicate these surpluses in some way, since there seems no requirement that those who create the surpluses should retain them. They are often actually created to be given to someone else, as in the potlatch ceremonies of the Native Americans of the Pacific Coast (Douglas and Isherwood, 1969). For many primitive peoples, the beneficiary was a god, often a sacred king, or the tribal ancestors. Even today, we shall see some instances where individuals earn surpluses and appear to retain them—but seem constrained by some neurotic urge from actually consuming them!

Because the physical form of the surplus is likely to be perishable, the need to transform its essence into something permanent has been felt from the earliest times. This is the primary purpose of money; its use as a medium of exchange is a quite modern development. Many less-developed cultures still exist in which the only use of money is for ceremonial purposes, such as the payment of a bride-price, blood-money, or the cost of funeral rites (Crump, 1981). This is why money is almost always something intrinsically worthless, such as stones, shells, feathers, or very soft metals—or paper. It must be made from materials that cannot be used for tools, or consumed; the use of cattle, or salt, as a medium of exchange is another quite recent development.

Money should also have distinctive eye-catching and/or tactile features, if it is to serve its sacramental purpose. This is to convey strictly ineffable ideas about 'goodness', or value, to the central nervous systems of those who handle it. Paper money and cheques might seem deficient in this respect; however, it is probable that the more social aspects of the rituals which *Homo sapiens* has developed around fiduciary issues of currency and negotiable instruments are sufficiently rich in *social* texture to compensate for the loss of the physical sight, sound and touch of cash itself.[1]

Because money is fundamental to civilization, society could not function without accounting. At the most primitive level, money is something which has to be taken care of. Stealing money is a more serious crime than stealing cattle, or other chattels; it is stealing a man's god. However, simple stewardship is overtaken by more complicated needs. As the social organization begins to grow beyond the extended family unit, the concept of debt emerges. Receiving a surplus confers status upon the recipient, and the resulting pecking-order plays an important part in breaking up the natural inability to distinguish 'self' and 'others' in one's own group. The basic purpose of money is as a means of transferring surpluses between subgroups. The main group could not cohere unless there is confidence that debts will be 'honoured', so the concept of solvency is basic to the social development of *Homo sapiens*.

'Advanced accounting' is also a necessary part of Level III common sense for a more basic reason. Because our rational models are based upon a restricted perception of reality, they appear to us to be admirably sharp-edged. For reasons which will be discussed in the next section of this chapter, we have a neurotic desire for logical 'closure' to our models. This drives us to construct them quite rigorously, although even 'mathematical precision' is an illusion of our conscious minds. Mathematics is anthropocentric; the Universe lies beyond our ideas of mathematics (Hofstadter, 1979). It follows that whatever common sense does to deconstruct our models back to reality cannot contravene the apparent mathematical closure of the model. Advanced accounting achieves this very neatly, by applying levitical precision to the measurement of phenomena analysed under very imprecise taxonomies. This permits us to engage in ritual negotiations about the model, accepting 'the figures' while debating the validity of the parameters which they represent.

To accept the ritual nature of accounting is not an act of intellectual nihilism. Accounts *do* convey information to the conscious intelligence of those who read them, as well as whatever common sense messages they may transmit to the central nervous system. The effect was well captured by

Sorter (1969), who contrasted what he described as the 'valuation' and the 'events' approaches to basic accounting theory. The people who adopted the former approach seemed to be seeking 'bottom lines', which involved some predetermined methods for measuring the wealth and net worth of an enterprise. There were others with the latter approach, whose concern was with the communication of market-sensitive information to investors, who made their own valuations, through the capital markets.

A possible explanation for the phenomenon is that the approaches represent two distinct systems of ideas which merely happen to coincide, loosely, in corporate financial reporting. The events approach to financial reporting would seem to be part of the larger corporate function of 'investor relations', or even 'public relations'. Moreover, accounting and finance involve internal as well as external reporting, and the same dichotomy would appear to exist with respect to managerial reports and statements. Probably the events approach, in its widest sense, should be seen as the philosophy underlying the entire 'corporate information' effort of the company. By contrast, the valuation approach seems to be a part of rituals which govern the psychological imperatives within the group of human collaborators who make up 'the corporation', and which provide the means by which they settle issues of relative status, claims against any surpluses and so on.[2]

Perhaps one could attempt a 'General Theory of Common Sense', along these lines. *All* observations and measurements, whether of natural or social phenomena, serve two functions. One is simply to convey information to the conscious intelligence, for use in its model of its environment. The other, common-sense use is to reconcile the human psyche to a Universe which it cannot properly perceive. For natural phenomena, the ritual, common-sense element is comparatively slight, although not insignificant.[3]

Accounting, Neurosis and Belief

Despite anthropological evidence of the origins of money and accounting, the proposition that there is a connection between modern accounting and finance on the one hand and religion on the other would seem strange to most people today. Many Western people would deny the existence of any god, while others would think that *their* God must be above sordid matters of trade, profit and loss. Others might be more disposed to accept that a religion might have an impact on the accounting practices of those who accept it, but probably only in the sense that, for a believer, religion might have an impact on everything. Accounting is another tool in the hands of men and women; the impact of religion on accounting would be much the same as its impact on a sewing machine. That is, it should affect what people do with it. The object of this chapter is to demonstrate that both views are incorrect. Accounting and 'faith' are inseparable, whatever one's belief, or supposed unbelief.

We have argued that our conscious minds formulate limited models, which are based on a limited capacity for observation. Moreover, every observation implies an overarching metascheme which supplies the taxonomy by which we can identify what it is that we observe. The metascheme can be overtly supernatural, as a theology, but any metascheme for producing knowledge of this kind requires a basic belief which is external to our own observation. This is the essence of the post-modernist approach to knowledge (Lyotard, 1984); one cannot avoid accepting some humanistic concept as 'real', and this must involve an 'act of faith'. For this limited purpose, of course, an acceptance of the fundamental assumptions of Newtonian physics, or neoclassical economics, is as valid as a belief in a god. Every metascheme involves measurement, valuation, classification, and even conservation as part of its definition of purpose. These features define accounting (Mattessich, 1964); indeed, accounting can have no purpose outside some metascheme of which some kind of faith is also an integral part.

Nevertheless, financial accounting is not readily associated with joyous affirmations of faith, whether in a supernatural or a natural order! Money and the need to account for it seem to embody the very spirit of acquisitiveness, fussy attention to detail, and distrust. This is unsurprising. A limitless pursuit of 'the good' is not necessarily a recipe for earthly happiness; it implies a basic dissatisfaction with what *is*. Genesis contrasts the happy state of Adam and Eve in the garden with their wiser but much less happy condition outside it. The great metascheme of Freudian psychology has an equally gloomy explanation of this development in Man. Freud defines civilization as a disease from which *Home sapiens* actually 'suffers'.

This theory suggests that since the period of childhood dependency lasts much longer in *Homo sapiens* than in other species, infantile sexuality is more deeply impressed upon us. As we grow up, society necessarily represses these instincts within us, in favour of more genetically productive ones. Since the infantile state is much concerned with physical sensation, this aspect of the theory confirms Gehlen's ideas of instinct reduction: our conscious repression of these sensations reinforces our ability to formulate abstract, limited models. This repression also reinforces our illusion of a separation between ourselves and our environment, and our belief that some states and actions are 'better' than others (Freud, 1950, 1969).

This led Freud to diagnose a basic, suppressed anal eroticism in both scientific and commercial endeavour. This is typified by a concern for precision, for acquisition and conservation, and above all by an illusion that one can stand apart from one's environment and manipulate it to advantage. A substantial literature, which covers several centuries, has explored this scatological analysis of human 'progress' (Brown, 1959). A belief in an obscene origin of this type of activity existed for many years before the formulation of Freudian psychoanalysis. The great Protestant Christian reformer, Martin Luther, expressed his ideas about the protocapitalism of his day, and the Catholic Church's tentative endorsement of its methods, largely in such terms, and unequivocally related them to the Devil. The next chapter recounts the subsequent development of the relationship between the Reformation and nascent capitalism in Europe and North America.

Evidence of a neurotic concern for precision, acquisition and conservation can be seen in much accounting activity. 'Maintenance of capital' is central to our ideas of economic profit, although we do not maintain the capital of any enterprise in practice. Commercial capital is expanded, contracted or maintained, as need or opportunity dictates. One might argue that, nevertheless, any significant measurement of business success would need a common base of this sort, but some very large enterprises go about their business without such statistics. Our central and local governments finance themselves on a year-to-year (or even a day-to-day) basis, through taxation and borrowing. As citizens we feel no urge to build up funds now, in order at some future time to replace the public assets which we currently enjoy.

If we cannot afford what we want in the public domain out of current income, we raise loans, which our successors as citizens will have to pay. Indeed, in business affairs also, we raise new capital, or loan capital, to finance any needs which cannot be met out of current cash-flow. There are limits beyond which both additional outside financing and the payment of dividends would be imprudent, for governments as well as for businesses. This is the case where their subsequent repayment, or even servicing, would immobilize too much of any likely future cash-flow, and so endanger the solvency of the entity. However, these limits are not closely related to economic income, as the case-law on divisible profits amply demonstrates. Freud might have said that we are very hard on ourselves as adult, individual business people, while as a group of citizens we bask in unthinking infantile self-gratification. As adult individuals, we seem to *need* to feel constricted, in finance as in much else, because it is only then that we can feel in control of our lives.

These more neurotic aspects of accounting and finance can be distinguished from the need for strict stewardship of money, and solvency. We have argued that the last two features of finance are necessary for the proper functioning of human society. As such, they are on a par with taboos such as incest-aversion (Lumsden and Wilson, 1981). Perhaps they should be called 'epicultural rules', in parallel with the epigenetic rules which Lumsden and Wilson suppose are needed to preserve the genetic inheritance. Epigenetic rules are taboos which *must* preserve and enhance the possibility of genetic survival without any chance of dictating an unwise action. As such, they can be imprinted directly into the unconscious mind, to surface as instinctive reactions.

'Rules' which can only be applied under appropriate circumstances must present themselves in the consciousness in order to allow opportunities for reflection. As such, they are no more than short cuts in the rational processes by which we decide what best to do. Their effect is to inhibit the range within which common sense can be used through advanced accounting, to deconstruct model solutions. To the extent that these inhibitions are invariably of a conservative, 'downside' type, they seem to be a measure of the level of neurosis in those who seek to apply them. Highly conservative personalities will be looking for strict and uniform levels of repression, as they do in all matters of inhibition; in dress, conversation, sexual behaviour and the rest.

Rituals, Institutions and Reality

Although we use ritual and sacraments, sacred and secular, to handle consciously inconceivable perceptions of reality, they have the same capacity to change that reality as has conscious observation. Just as the Christian sacrament of the Mass requires bread, wine, chalices, priests, vestments, buildings, together with a managerial structure to provide and coordinate these things, the secular sacraments also have to be reified in instruments and institutions. These institutional 'outward and visible signs' promote social cohesion (March and Olsen, 1980), but they also have the secondary effect of compelling participants' actions to conform with the cultural norms, whatever their personal beliefs. The existence of markets actually ensures that the goods we need are in short supply (Lamb, 1982), while the existence of Western-style banks gives money a tangible time-value among those who choose, or are compelled, to use them. However, since the institutions and the rituals themselves can be seen to vary from place to place, and also over time, one might wonder whether a given ritual was in the best form for its current purposes.

Neither religious nor secular social theoreticians are ever proactive, in the sense of inventing new ways of worship, making money, or even presenting accounts (Watts and Zimmerman, 1979; Gambling, 1987).[4] Instead, they incorporate new 'popular devotions' into orthodox belief and practice, or anathematize them. The emergence of new economic devotions, in the shape of new forms of business organization, financing or trading, must be our common-sense reactions to changes in the underlying realities of the Universe. Some of those changes will be due to actions brought about by earlier sacraments. It would not be useful to suppose that primary common-sense reactions are 'more epicultural' than secondary ones, since evolutionary changes can be neither good nor bad in themselves. On the other hand, evolutionary changes can be dead-ends for the species concerned, as the dinosaurs and dodos would testify. Since we have free will to embrace or reject changes in ritual, we might consider possible evidences of a 'good ritual' for the purposes of communicating common sense *and* promoting social cohesion.

The primary purpose of ritual is communication through the senses. A good ritual might be expected to exhibit a degree of sensuality! It should involve actual, close personal contact; the handling of documents, equipment and, indeed, of other people; if possible, the exercising of the whole range of the senses in what is going on. The proposition that organizations could be run largely through the use of remote computer terminals seems unlikely, if only for this reason. The secondary purpose is the promotion of organizational stability. Since both conventional religion and modern cosmology suggest that the Universe provides a reasonably stable and supportive environment, life-enhancing rituals ought not to disturb the natural order. Any organization experiencing continual destabilization should look to its pattern of rituals. Finally, ritual consumes time and materials. If its proliferation is unchecked, it is likely that ritual will consume resources better devoted to productive or defensive activity. Since common sense is an unconscious phenomenon, it is not possible to be certain of the point at which ceremonial goes into excess, but a massive growth of involved 'Byzantine' administrative cadres must always be viewed with suspicion.[5]

The successful adoption of so-called 'world-class manufacturing' techniques in Japan and elsewhere illustrates these issues. Paperwork and computer terminals are massively reduced, so the management functions 'by walking about'. Managers and workers are involved in continual social interaction on the shop-floor, surrounded by and touching, hearing and smelling the machine tools and the materials in process. The production track is the scene of continuous hands-on experimentation as to manning levels, maintenance, layout and product design. The result appears to be a more immediate and more accurate application of common sense to the manufacturing process, unimpeded by the need for management reports and control systems, staff functionaries and the other features of a manufacturing bureaucracy (Schonberger, 1986).

Theistic versus Atheistic Faith

The psychological/neurological analysis of human social activity adopted in this chapter is neutral as between religion and humanism. If God existed, He would not see Himself as a magician! The Universe 'works' mechanically, even if its 'real' mechanics are beyond the grasp of *Homo sapiens*. We have found it necessary to consider these issues of psychology and neurology because they seem to provide the broadest metascheme, including an explanation of the function of accounting and finance in society. We have argued that some act of faith must underpin every metascheme for human intelligence, while observing that 'rationalist' faiths are entirely feasible. In those areas where Level III common sense operates, this involves the construction of a set of criteria for human action which is external to the individual, but effective for society as a whole—in short, a social science. Our next chapter describes how these ideas emerged in eighteenth- and early-nineteenth-century Europe. Nevertheless, we need to conclude the present chapter by saying something about the moral dimensions of the choice between a religious and a humanistic approach to life—and hence to business and accounting.

The basic tenet of economic theory is that Man is driven by self-interest, in a world where resources are in short supply. This assumption is at variance with modern cosmology, as well with the doctrine of most of the major religions of the world. Economic theory can be viewed as the theology of a secular faith in the Economizing Spirit of Man. As such, it exhibits at least one feature not found in more spiritual codes of belief. It has taken its fundamental assumptions exclusively from the most 'civilized' and hence the most neurotic elements in the human condition: the desire to stand apart from others, to compete, to manipulate, and to amass surpluses. This is inevitable in any professedly 'rational' theory, which can only recognize the conscious elements in human intelligence. It must ignore all those life-preserving and life-enhancing elements which human beings share with the social animals, and which present themselves unconsciously to the central nervous system as common sense.

Trade and administration are our methods of pursuing 'the good', while accounting is the method by which we keep the score for our efforts to 'be good'. Many people find it difficult to see as 'being good' the relentless pursuit of surpluses of what they value. This merely demonstrates the extent to which the economizing spirit has succeeded in relegating all concerns for morality to the realms of philosophy, and the home. The goodness of a good father is not to be measured by the same standards used for 'a good businessman'. This is illogical: if the standards are not the same, they will eventually be in conflict, when the individual is faced with a decision whose outcome will be good for fatherhood and bad for business, or vice versa. In practice, this is the type of dilemma which has to be resolved by the use of common sense, through the appropriate social rituals.

On the other hand, it is a wholly artificial dilemma, of comparatively recent origin. The following chapter will show that this convenient dichotomy was not available to business people in former times. We shall also see the curious developments of moral philosophy which led to its creation. Of course, those who want to create Islamic States entirely obedient to the Shari'a are proposing to dispense with it altogether. Some people would argue that the dichotomy is a useful extension of 'instinct reduction' by social scientists, on a par with the equally artificial concept of 'scientific detachment' adopted by natural science. Others, including the authors, would think the use of a limited *morality* less than truly human. 'Knowing good and evil' is the mark of humanity, and our understanding of those qualities is amplified by Platonism, if not by revealed religion. We know that standards of 'good' are not divisible; to suppose that common sense can deconstruct models constructed on a contrary principle is to identify common sense with Adam Smith's 'Divine Hand of Providence'. We can see no grounds for supposing that it is efficient, or even possible, to look for instinct reduction plus common sense to replicate moral imperatives which are already perfectly well known to the human consciousness.

Notes

1. Here is an example of negotiable instruments perceived as totemic symbols, in Hollywood in the 1940s and 1970s:

It was the beginning of a whole new financial period in Hollywood, that of the modern 'deal'—the symbolic big money on paper that means the dealer is moving up (or staying there). Joan Didion described the magical property such numbers had acquired by 1973:

> The action itself is an art form, and is described in aesthetic terms: 'A very imaginative deal,' they say, or, 'He writes the most creative deals in the business.' . . . I talk on the telephone to an agent, who tells me that he has on his desk a check made out to a client for $1,275,000, the client's share of the first profits on a movie now in release. Last week, in someone's office I was shown another such check, this one made out for $4,850,000. Every year there are a few such checks around town. An agent will speak of such a check as being 'on my desk', or 'on Guy McIlwaine's desk', as if the exact physical location lent the piece of paper its credibility . . . the actual pieces of paper which bear such numbers have, in the community, a totemic significance. They are totems of the action. (Didion, 1980, pp. 158–9, in Wills, 1988)

2. Here is an example, taken from a nineteenth-century military enquiry into some regimental accounts:

5. Besides the above current accounts, Lieutenant Hodson, soon after taking command of the regiment, caused a transcript of the available Persian records to be made by one Moonshee Bachee Lall in the Hindi character. This transcript was set about with the express object of obtaining a more correct and detailed knowledge of all previous transactions than was furnished by the accounts which had been kept first by Lieutenant Hawes (in English) and then by his successor, Lieutenant Turner (in Persian), which though good records of the receipts and disbursements which had passed through the hands of those officers, were no evidence of the real financial state of the regiment, as they had never been balanced periodically, and when made over furnished no detail of the balance in hand.

6. It was, then, in the hope of thoroughly clearing the account from end to end, and obtaining a detail of the balance for which he was liable, that Lieutenant Hodson set Moonshee Bachee Lall to work at his transcript of the accounts, and he first wrote out the cash-book kept by Subadar Peer Buksh, then that by Munawar Allee under Lieutenant Turner's supervision, then Nujjuf Allee's own, the transcript of which, after being brought up to date, was continued from day to day as a check.

7. An attempt to complete a *khata*, or balanced account from Peer Buksh's daybook failed (Trotter, 1901, p. 270).

It is clear that in addition to the hope of discovering the balance on the regimental imprest for which he had accepted liability, Lieutenant Hodson was relying on the preparation of a ritually clean set of records to demonstrate his financial probity.

3. For social phenomena, however, the element of ritual is far higher than our conscious minds find it congenial to accept. This has been demonstrated by Morgenstern (1964), who shows that most social and economic statistics are exceedingly unreliable. He suggests that the same must be true of accounting data as well. The margin of error reported by Morgenstern is sufficiently gross to support the contention that the data are intended for use in (ritual) negotiations, rather than direct

indications of courses of action. This 'propagation of error' in calculations is well known to physicists (Jaech, 1985; Topping, 1955), but seems almost unremarked in the social sciences (Gambling, 1975). This again is unsurprising, if one can accept the idea of the common-sense use of figures in the rituals of daily life.

4. The conjunction of these outwardly very different references from Western accounting theory suggests that the societal theory of accounting is sufficiently robust to encompass positive economics and religion! Gambling examines the (secular) ritual nature of accounting, while Watts and Zimmerman demonstrated how particular varieties of accounting ritual will be commonly associated with particular types of entities. The series of historical references adduced by Watts and Zimmerman also provide substantial support for the proposition that fresh developments in accounting emerge as part of a popular devotion, rather than from any conscious attempts to improve the design of a technique.

5. The adjective 'Byzantine' refers to the elaborate, involved court-ceremonials which were a principal feature of the administration of the Eastern capital of the Roman Empire at Byzantium. By coincidence, it was the debility of this empire in the seventh and eighth centuries which facilitated the growth of Islam in most of its former territories (see the Appendix to Chapter 2).

Bibliography

Ali Abdullah Yusuf, *The Holy Qur-ran: Text, Translation and Commentary* (Beirut: Dar Al Arabia, 1968).

Arnold, M. E., T. E. Gambling and D. G. Rush, 'Expert Systems: As Expert as the Accountants?'. *Management Accounting (UK)*, Vol. 63 (1985), pp. 20–2.

Barrow, J. D., and F. J. Tipler, *The Anthropic Cosmological Principle* (Oxford: Oxford University Press, 1986).

Brown, N. O., *Life against Death: The Psychoanalytical Meaning of History* (Middleton, Conn.: Wesleyan University Press, 1959).

Capra, Fritjof, *The Tao of Physics* (New York: Random House, 1975).

Chase, W. G., and H. A. Simon, 'The Mind's Eye in Chess', *in* W. G. Chase (Ed.), *Visual Information Processing* (New York: Academic Press, 1973), pp. 215–81.

Cleverley, Graham, *Managers and Magic* (London: Penguin, 1973).

Crump, Thomas, *The Phenomenology of Money* (London: Routledge & Kegan Paul, 1981).

Didion, Joan, *The White Album* (New York: Pocket Books, 1980).

Douglas, M., and B. Isherwood, *The World of Goods: Towards an Anthropology of Consumption* (Oxford: Allen Lane, 1969).

Dreyfus, H., and S. E. Dreyfus, *Mind over Matter: The Power of Human Intuition and Expertise in the Era of the Computer* (Oxford: Blackwell, 1986).

Eich, J. M., 'A Computer Holographic Associative Recall Memory', *Psychological Review*, Vol. 89 (1982), pp. 627–61.

Freud, Sigmund, *Beyond the Pleasure Principle* (J. Strachey, translator), (London: Hogarth Press, 1950).

——, *Collected Papers, Vol. II* (Joan Riviere, translator), (London: Hogarth Press, 1969).

Gambling, Trevor, *Societal Accounting* (London: Allen & Unwin, 1974).

——, *Modern Accounting: Accounting as the Information System for Technological Change* (London: Macmillan, 1975).

——, *Positive Accounting: Problems and Solutions* (London: Macmillan, 1984).

——, 'Expert Systems: Stone Age Rules, OK?', *Accountancy*, Vol. 96 (1985), pp. 125–7.

——, 'Accounting for Rituals', *Accounting, Organizations and Society*, Vol. 12 (1987), pp. 319–29.

Hayes, P. J., 'The Naive Physics Manifesto', *in* D. Michie (Ed.), *Expert Systems in the Micro-electronic Age* (Edinburgh: Edinburgh University Press, 1979), pp. 242–70.

Hofstadter, Douglas M., Gödel, *Escher, Bach: An Eternal Golden Braid* (London: Harvester Press, 1979).

Jaech, J. I., *Statistical Analysis of Measurement Errors* (New York: Wiley, 1985).

Lamb, M. I., *Solidarity with Victims* (New York: Crossroad, 1982).

Lumsden, C. J., and E. O. Wilson, *Genes, Mind and Culture* (Cambridge, Mass.: Harvard University Press, 1981).

Lyotard, Jean, *The Postmodern Condition: A Report on Knowledge* (G. Bennington and B. Massumi, translators), (Minneapolis, Minn.: University of Minnesota Press, 1984).

March, J. G., and J. P. Olsen, *Ambiguity and Choice in Organizations*, 2nd edition (Oxford: Oxford University Press, 1980).

Mattessich, Richard, *Accounting and Analytical Methods: Measure and Projection of Income and Wealth in Micro- and Macro-economy* (Homewood, Ill.: Irwin, 1964).

Morgenstern, O., *On the Accuracy of Economic Observations*, 2nd edition (Princeton, N.J.: Princeton University Press, 1964).

Peter, Karl, and Nicholas Petryszak, 'Sociobiology versus Biosociology', *in* Ashley Montague (Ed.), *Sociobiology Examined* (New York: Oxford University Press, 1980), pp. 39–81.

Ròheim, G., *The Eternal Ones of the Dream: A Psychoanalytic Interpretation of Australian Myth and Ritual* (Independence, Mo.: International University Press, 1945).

Schonberger, R. J., *World Class Manufacturing: The Lessons of Simplicity Applied* (New York: The Free Press, 1986).

Sorter, G. H., 'An "Events" Approach to Basic Accounting Theory', *The Accounting Review*, Vol. 44 (1969), pp. 12–19.

Thomas, Arthur L., *The Allocation Problem in Financial Accounting Theory: AAA Studies in Accounting Theory No. 3* (Sarasota, Fla.: American Accounting Association, 1969).

Topping, J., *Errors of Observation and Their Treatment* (London: Chapman & Hall, 1955).

Trotter, Lionel J., *The Life of Hodson of Hodson's Horse* (London: Dent, 1901).

Watts, Ross L., and Jerold L. Zimmerman, 'The Demand for and Supply of Accounting Theories: The Market for Excuses', *The Accounting Review*, Vol. 54 (1979), pp. 273–305.

Wills, Garry, *Reagan's America: Innocents at Home* (London: Heinemann, 1988).

Chapter 2

Islam and Capitalism

The History of Religious Control of Business

Since Islam advocates a complete code of human conduct, it contains a number of directives which apply to the conduct of business and administrative affairs. The latter part of this chapter attempts to summarize these requirements. Although Islam has been one of the major faiths of the world for over thirteen centuries, as yet Muslims have not been able to develop a specifically Islamic body of accounting theory. This situation has resulted from the problems of developing large-scale, capital-intensive business activity in the Middle East in previous centuries. These difficulties seem to have been inherent in the political structure of the area in those days, which is now completely changed. The appendix to this chapter says something of the history of the Middle East as it appears to have affected business development.

On the other hand, capital-intensive investment has been possible for many years in other parts of the world, but no Christian (or Buddhist, or Marxist) accounting theory has developed in those places either. Accounting must always involve some sort of faith, but it is the secular economizing spirit which is applied to business and administration everywhere in the world. It might seem that those present-day Muslims who propose to create truly Islamic societies have no role-models for the application of religious faith to business, and hence to accounting.

This is not so. The Christian Church in Europe made consistent and well-documented attempts to enforce canon law in business affairs, for many centuries. It was the growth of modern, large-scale capitalism which brought about the Church's eventual failure to enforce religious discipline in this area and, finally, the total abandonment of business to the secular economizing spirit. There are extensive similarities between the rules for

22

business laid down by Christian canon law and those contained in the Islamic Shariʻa. It seems reasonable to suppose that the difficulties which defeated canon law in the past will also be those which are likely to cause major problems for those seeking to impose the Shariʻa today. The first part of this chapter describes those difficulties.

It is only in the last three centuries or thereabouts that the Western churches have accepted that business was an activity beyond their direct control. Before that date, commerce was seen as a matter of morality, and subject to divine ordinances. Every branch of Christendom provided more or less detailed directives as to what God's Law for the prosecution of trade and industry might be. To be sure, there were violent disputes between the subscribers to the many religious authorities who ventured into this field. The works of St Thomas Aquinas, St Antoninus of Florence, Luther, Calvin, Knox and Baxter were used in their various times to justify or denounce the strategems by which the Western business community sought to make its conduct a matter for self-regulation—or even for regulation by perceived natural law.

The economic history of that period was the subject of controversy at the beginning of the present century. This originated in the publication of Weber's two papers on 'The Protestant Ethic and the Spirit of Capitalism' (1904, 1905), and largely subsided after the appearance of Tawney's *Religion and the Rise of Capitalism* (1926). Weber had observed how the most explosive development of modern capitalism had occurred among French émigrés in sixteenth-century Geneva, and thereafter among Puritan communities in England, Scotland and New England. These were people who subscribed to the fundamentalist Protestant theology of Jean Calvin. Weber's hypothesis was that 'the spirit of capitalism' was fostered by Calvin's extreme interpretation of Martin Luther's concept of 'a Christian calling'.

Weber supposed that this was a product of Luther's rejection of the institution of Christian monasticism. Formerly, lay-people (and secular priests) were believed to be bound by less strict rules of life than those to be observed by monks and nuns. The superior performance of those in religious orders was seen as compensating in some degree for less exalted behaviour in other walks of life. Therefore, in the absence of any religious orders, the Protestant lay-person's 'calling' was to follow a rule of life of the highest order. One's daily work could be and should be conducted in the strictest obedience to God's commandments; the humblest type of work undertaken in this spirit was more acceptable to God than a lifetime of spiritual exercises. Calvin (said Weber) was the first reformer to attach these ideas formally to *trading*. This led his followers to exalt the pursuit of business to the exclusion of all else, a belief that worldly success was evidence of divine grace—and eventually to a belief that self-interest and God's interest were interdependent!

History does not often support such popular analyses of the influences of 'great men'. Tawney, and other commentators, could demonstrate that well-known, substantial Catholic theologians had been aware of, and even approved, similar theories about God's favour to the astute businessman long before Calvin arrived in Geneva. Again, while the English-speaking Calvinists in the seventeenth and eighteenth centuries may have effectively replaced God by Mammon, this was not the case in sixteenth-century Geneva. There, Calvin's doctrines resulted in a form of Christian socialism. Moreover, many English Calvinists of the earlier part of the seventeenth century were led to form groups such as the Levellers and the Diggers, who practised a primitive form of communism.

The Rise of Capitalism

Calvinism could not have caused 'the rise of capitalism', or even have originated the attitudes of mind which produced it. These had been developing over many years, as canon law became less able to encompass the growth of economic activity in medieval Europe. The emergence of Islam was itself part of this process, in so far as it made it possible to expand trade with the Far East along the Danube valley. The discovery of the Americas was another factor which produced levels and styles of economic activity which could not be contained by a law framed for an unchanging, agrarian society of the feudal type. Calvin's ideas found support among communities which most desired to break out of the traditional mould, and so strengthened the movement toward a self-justifying capitalism in those areas where embryo capitalists were most numerous. The value of the controversy over Weber's thesis for this book is the light it throws on how 'modern' large-scale capitalism functioned in Europe *before* the development of a purely secular economic theory (*see* Green, 1959).

The medieval canon law, like the Shari'a, held the taking and payment of interest on loans to be a major sin. The only way to put capital to work was as a sole proprietor, or as a partner. Thus, the capitalist had to accept some risk of loss, and, ideally, should contribute in running the business. Ecclesiastical authorities prosecuted people for usury all over Europe until well into the fifteenth century. However, money-lenders often found powerful protectors. Princes and municipal corporations both found it useful to bor-

24

row large sums at interest, without the need to make the lenders partners in their affairs. The obvious differences between the circumstances of such loans and those of loans to peasants and small traders suggested a less rigorous interpretation of the laws against usury. It was loans to the poor and ignorant which are offensive to God; wealthy and educated people are well able to take care of themselves.

This sophistry could find support in some ideas which were central to the medieval concept of society. A society was like a body, each of whose members had different functions contributing to the welfare of the whole. The various members had a pre-ordained 'station in life', which entitled them to different standards of living. There was also an assumption that the amount of sustenance available overall was of fixed amount. If any member exacts more than its ordained share, the other members of the body must have their rights diminished, to the detriment of the whole. From this emerged the concept of 'the just price', which was the amount necessary to keep the producer according to his or her station of life. Moreover, in a closed system where everybody had just enough to keep going at the appropriate level, nobody could accumulate a surplus to lend, except by extortion.

This view of the world is invalidated at any points where the system is, in fact, open. The external policies of princes, or international traders, did not encroach upon the living-space of fellow men and women *within* their society. Again, technological developments in agriculture and manufacture produce surpluses in a society, without extortion. Any dealings which are confined to external trade, or surplus-creation, cannot be oppressing more traditional peasants and artisans. These arguments imply that the society is traditional, for the most part, where only a very small minority of people make external contacts, or undertake innovation. Given that, one might believe that courses of trading could be usurious in some circumstances, but good banking practice in others.

The Breakdown of Canon Law in Europe

Another precondition of the medieval view of society was that the majority of the people accepted their traditional place—and life at a subsistence level. This depended on their acceptance that they could not better their lot, other than by destroying their society. The effect of the events already mentioned—increased trade with the Far Fast, the discovery of the Americas, and innovations in farming and manufacturing—cannot actually be confined to the minorities who first develop them. They become diffused throughout society, more or less rapidly. When common soldiers and sailors come home with more gold than they can carry, and small artisans become as rich as noblemen, it is not easy to believe in a God-given order which dictates one's place in society. It seemed to many Europeans of those times that if the social order could change so greatly, the truth of concepts like the just price and the evils of usury had ceased to be self-evident.

Another response to such changes might be to suppose that change itself was an evil. It is an irony that the Christian Reformation, which is now seen to have a central place in the development of modern capitalism, had its origins in a protest against social and economic change! This fact has already been referred to in Chapter 1, since the great reformer, Martin Luther, made the dubious psychological foundations of the pursuit of money a keystone in his arguments for the reform of the Church. The original Protestant movement was, in fact, agrarian and quite antagonistic towards business enterprise; it was also opposed to innovation in agriculture itself. A number of Lutheran sectarians (such as the Amish) removed themselves to the New World for the express purpose of avoiding the so-called 'agricultural revolution'. To this day, their descendants refuse to use farm machinery, artificial fertilizers, etc. and organize their lives in the most traditional peasant fashion. It may be a further example of the irony attaching to the human condition that the Amish ideal of peasant farming did not extend to an endorsement of the land-tenure laws of sixteenth-century Bohemia; the Amish came to the New World to effect a social reform of their own.

'Business is Business'

Those Europeans who did accept the possibility that God had no objection to social change were still faced with the problem of assessing whether any one change in the existing order was for good or bad. In the event, Western Man came to the conclusion that no judgement was necessary, because the socio-economic system is self-regulating. By happy chance, the system is driven by naked human greed. In the long run, those who try to take advantage of their neighbours are brought back into line by market forces. 'Man's self-interest is God's providence.' Modern analysis may find the proposition hypocritical, but it is not easy to dismiss the apparent sincerity with which the view was held in its time. Tawney and the other contributors to the controversy over the 'Protestant ethic' show *how* an abundantly fervent movement for Christian reform came to be diverted into this arid channel. They do not consider *why* the idea had so much popular appeal in an 'Age of Faith'. Nor do they pursue its development into the secular economic theory of the 'Age of Reason' in the eighteenth and nineteenth centuries.

It may be that these writers have tended to overlook the part played in these developments by simple anti-clericalism. Those of us who live in societies where religion has been confined to more domestic aspects of piety find it hard to imagine life where religion encompasses both economics and politics. Medieval Europeans were ignorant, for the most part, but they were able to observe that they were being oppressed by their noble landlords in the name of social stability. They were also aware that the Christian Church seemed to endorse the system as God-given. Peasants' revolts against landlord and parson were the seed-bed of the Protestant reformation, but even where the reformation succeeded, the net result left the common people with new landlords and new parsons to support the *status quo ante*. A strong body of opinion throughout Europe actually opposed *any* system whereby either a Catholic priest or a Protestant minister should be the arbiter of right and wrong in economic matters.

Chapter 1 of this book has shown how any admission of a limit to human rational perception creates a largely untestable 'black box' which has to be bridged by faith. Since Christian tradition has always endorsed the idea of priesthood, it is difficult for anyone brought up in that tradition to imagine a faith without some caste of experts in belief. We shall discuss the Islamic tradition in this matter a little later in this chapter. In Europe, ministers like Calvin, and later Baxter in England, attempted to reconcile their basically anti-clerical flocks to ecclesiastic discipline in business matters by matching their essential unbelief with doctrines of sophisticated pliability. However, these ideas were rapidly overtaken by the dawn of the Age of Reason, which took the fundamental position that human rationality must represent the final limit of knowledge. Humanism permitted the development of the utilitarian philosophies from which a purely secular 'science of political economy' could develop at the end of the eighteenth century.

It is beyond the scope of this book to consider how well purely secular economizing has worked since its emergence in the eighteenth century. Probably one could say that both *laissez-faire* capitalism and its Marxian counterpart of national economic planning have 'worked' about as well as the old canon law system can be said to have worked. People have survived, for the most part; social changes have taken place; standards of living, and perhaps even standards of civilization, may have advanced slightly overall. However, the advance is very uneven, and it has been achieved at the cost of great upheaval and unhappiness.

The Islamic Alternative

No one has yet attempted to regulate economic affairs in a modern economy in accordance with the teachings of Islam. It follows that the question whether Islam would work as well as these other systems, or actually surpass them, must be a matter of faith. However, it is important to appreciate that Islam differs in one major respect from both Christianity and humanism. Christianity sees *Homo sapiens* as a fallen creature, while humanism supposes that Man is by nature a rampant egoist. Secular economizing assumes that this self-interest can either regulate itself, or be controlled by the superior vision of political *illuminati*. Islam takes as its starting-point the tenet that men and women are *naturally* committed to be good. This strikes at the heart of humanism; in particular, neoclassical economics has nothing to say about the behaviour of those with a potentially self-sacrificing commitment to some course of action (Sen, 1976–7).

By accepting the possibility of personal commitment, Islam rejects the possibility of a separation between religious and temporal affairs. However, this does not mean that Islam calls for a theocratic state, at least in the sense of one that is dominated by a priestly caste. Priests, as understood in other religions, do not exist in Islam. All people are equal in the sight of God, and have direct access to Him. Mullahs and ayatollahs are essentially no more than someone chosen to lead the public prayers in a mosque on a regular basis. Current events and the past history of Muslim countries nevertheless suggest that 'religious leaders' often play a major part in public life! There is no contradiction in this, since religion is central to the life of a Muslim, and the Qur'an teaches that men of knowledge are especially honoured (39:9).

Such people are especially valued in Islamic society anyway, by reason of the nature of Islam itself. It differs from other religions in that it is primarily a divinely inspired political and economic system. The sacred writings have comparatively little to say about the nature of God and His angels, or indeed anything except human behaviour; it follows that Islam has no theology, as it is understood in other faiths. The principles governing the system (known as *usul*) are to 'be found in the Qur'an, which sets out the revealed Word of God, and *al-Hadith*, which are the personal teachings of the Prophet Mohammed. These principles constitute the Islamic Shari'a, and have to be obeyed, under all temporal and spatial conditions. However, the sacred texts do not set out 'the law' in a secular, statutory form; Muslim states have to incorporate these basic principles into their own legislation, in the normal way.

This is not always an easy task, whether the responsibility of framing the legislation rests with a prince or with a democratic legislature. Many of the teachings are in fairly general terms, and every Muslim is left to exercise discretion (*ijtihad*) over how best to implement these. This is not a matter of personal choice, however; its criteria and purpose should be the public interest of the whole community (*ummah*). This flexibility enables Muslims to adapt to changing conditions and environments, and contrasts with Christian canon law in this respect. As in other legal codes, earlier exercises of *ijtihad* form precedents for future decisions. It follows that Islam has always had a body of jurists (*ulama*) who were held to be experts in the complexities of the Shari'a. It should be noted that these experts have not always agreed on these matters, and it is possible to distinguish a number of schools of thought on a wide variety of such issues.

This is as it should be, because Islam does not value conservatism for its own sake. We shall see that it is a fundamental principle of Islam that anybody can express an opinion on the interpretation of the Shari'a principles; indeed, this book is itself such an expression. In the same way, everybody is entitled to solicit the support of others for his or her point of view, and attempt to influence the form of the legislation. Nevertheless, the extent to which this right should be exercised by lay-people is a matter of contention in modern Islam, as it has been for a very large part of Islamic history.

The Law and the Lawyers in Islam

The difference of opinion is fundamental: humanly speaking, it could well confound the current attempts at Islamic revival through the establishment of Islamic States. Although Islam needs no priesthood, as such, the need for strict obedience to a code of law whose principles alone are laid down in the Qur'an means that one *could* suppose that the detail of the law ought to be construed from case law going back to the time of the Prophet, and the *Ijtihad* Period. Clearly, this is a professional expertise, which requires the professional education and training of an (ecclesiastical) lawyer. In a general way, it might seem appropriate for lay-persons to refer all such issues to the *ulama*—and follow their advice. Such an approach is feasible. The giving of advice which is very likely to be taken is not something which should be undertaken lightly. While Muslims must make up their own minds as to whether they agree with the propriety of the advice, any wrongdoing caused by those who decide to accept it is the personal responsibility of the original proposer of the interpretation. The moral responsibility of influential religious leaders in Islam is very substantial.

On the other hand, an equally defensible view might be that if God had wanted to lay down the detail of the Shari'a, He would have done so directly. The fact that He did not choose to do so means that the faithful continually have to search for indications of God's will, one way of doing so being by asking the advice of more experienced persons. This is the purpose of the *al-Istikhara* prayer, in which Muslims are supposed to seek God's guidance before major decisions. This should not be construed as an invitation to practise 'situation ethics'; as was said in the Introduction, Muslims do not appeal to an 'inner light' of conscience against the Law. The Law is a complete and sufficient guide to human behaviour, and there is only one correct course of action in any circumstance. However, God does not set His people historical puzzles, and will let the sincere seeker for guidance know what the Law requires him or her to do.

Because of their emphasis on spiritual legitimacy (*Imamah*), the Shi'ites tend to oppose debate between lay-persons and the *ulama* over interpretation of Shari'a principles. This issue is central to an understanding of current developments in Iran:

> while the authority to interpret the law and express opinions on questions of religious practice has been traditionally reserved to the jurists, one outcome of the tendency to articulate political issues in the language of Islam, is that laymen have begun to appropriate to themselves the authority to interpret religious texts and the sources of the law. (Bakhash, 1988, p. 32)

It is probable that many Muslims would join in condemning the more extreme rejection of the jurists' authority. The European experience described in the first part of this chapter shows how the growth of enthusiasm for lay interpretation of canon law led inexorably toward a secular society.

The problem, we believe, is that mentioned in Chapter 1: theologians tend to be reactive, rather than proactive, in such matters. As circumstances change in the outside world, those in daily contact with the problems created by change quite naturally form ideas as to what should be done to deal with them. If they approach the jurists at that point in time, the latter can only agree wholly or in part with what they have in mind, or forbid it. Such is the nature of Man as a political animal that this procedure is likely to drive the jurists' position toward that of the lay-people rather than vice versa. In a general way, as we have argued, Islam should be better placed than Christianity to handle social and technological change. Islam does not commend a static agricultural society, nor does it admit situation ethics. It is only the necessary ignorance about the day-to-day practice of business, etc. on the part of the specialist lawyer which is the cause of the problem.

However, there is an old-established branch of secular law which seems capable of adaptation to securing a more effective interface between jurists and lay-people in an Islamic society. This is known as administrative law, and involves the setting up of groups of 'commissioners' to exercise their discretion in the administration of limited areas of activity, subject to some basic legislation laying down the principles within which they must carry out their duties (Allen, 1965; Davis, 1971). Typical areas are the licensing of market-traders and taxi-cabs, airlines and commercial television stations. Chapter 3 will show that this arrangement existed in the early Muslim State, where a *sahib al-suq* was appointed to ensure that the market-traders conformed to the Shari'a in their dealings. This appointment demonstrates the essential element in administrative law: the commissioners should be independent of the activity they control, but in day-to-day contact with it. The Shari'a committees in the Islamic banks are something of this sort, although they are 'in-house' appointments.

Our own advocacy of lay discussion of the application of the Shari'a principles to modern, large-scale business does not extend to self-regulation, even where 'outside' jurists are involved in the process. The difficulties of this approach are discussed at length in Chapter 3. Nevertheless, since every lay-person with a concern for any field of interest has a right, and even a duty, to express an opinion about it, it is in this spirit that we offer our contribution to the debate.

This personal responsibility for the giving and taking of advice is enhanced by the belief among Muslims that Islam is not a matter of choice and conversion. Islam (as they see it) is nothing less than the Maker's instructions on how to operate as a human being. One does not *become* a Muslim, because every man and woman was born into that state. Instead one comes to a realization of that fact, and makes a declaration of it. People who do not profess to be Muslims either do not realize what they are, or prefer to ignore it. This means that Islam is universal, in time and space (Qutb, 1953; Al-Faruqi, 1979). According to Al-Faruqi:[1]

> Islam asserts that the territory of the Islamic State is the whole earth, or better the whole cosmos since the possibility of space travel is not too remote. . . . Its citizenry need not be all Muslims. What is important is that the citizenry include all those human beings who agree to live under the auspices of the Islamic State because they approve of its order and policies. (Al-Faruqi, 1979, pp. 61–2)

31

The Basic Principles of Islamic Political Economy

This concept of Islam as a natural order of things, which is already in place throughout the Universe, explains the expectation of total commitment from a Muslim. There is no heroic struggle to overcome one's natural weaknesses involved in being a good Muslim. It lies within the power of every man and woman on earth who will simply follow the dictates of conscience. This also explains the unashamedly Utopian nature of this book: if one rejects the assumptions of the fallen, or brutal, nature of Man, it may be a useful exercise to consider how individuals and states might be expected to function where a positive commitment to virtue is the norm.

This is what Islam professes, and the result is a highly integrated set of basic rules for personal and public life which makes no provision whatever for 'situational ethics'. This book is concerned with the economic activities of Muslims, but their (ideal) economic system is so closely interwoven with their political system that it makes no sense to discuss the one without the other. Qutb (1953) argues that the Islamic economic system should be viewed from a holistic perspective which involves an understanding of the concept of God, the Universe, life and the human being. This holistic approach provides an appreciation of the nature of social justice in Islam. The essential tenets of the Islamic political system are said to be:

1. God's unity and supreme sovereignty (*tawhid*).
2. Justice on the part of the ruler (*adalah*).
3. Obedience from the community (*bay'a*).
4. Free consultation between the ruler and the community (*shura*) (Qutb, 1953).
5. Succession (*khilafa*)—another important institution in the Islamic State. This covers the legitimacy of anyone's claim to own, or rule, anything at all. Since God is supreme, Man's role as an owner or ruler is that of 'God's viceregent on earth'. The political implications refer to the process by which any form of government has come into power, and the scope of its authority. More will be said about the economic implications of *khilafa* directly.

The last-named issue has been the source of conflict between the two main Muslim sects, the Sunni and the Shi'ites. The latter use the term *imamah*, rather than *khilafa*, to include both religious and political legitimacy dimensions in a true ruler. The former do not seem to require any particular religious legitimacy (Ismael and Ismael, 1985), and *khilafa* is based upon (Umarah, 1977):

1. Consultation (*shura*).

2. Choice, or election (*ikhtiyar*).
3. Contract (*aqid*).
4. Allegiance (*bay'a*).

According to Ahmad (1930, p. 230), the Islamic economic system is built on the following basic philosophical foundations, which largely overlap with those underlying the political system:[2]

1. *Tawhid*, but with the emphasis on God's ultimate ownership of all wealth.
2. *Khilafa*, which here refers more specifically to the rules governing the possession and disposal of property. One of the principles on which the Islamic economic system is built is that individuals have the right of private ownership (Audah, 1977; Qutb, 1953). This right is protected so long as the means of acquisition is lawful. Unlawful means of acquiring wealth include usury (including the taking of interest) (Qur'an 2:278–9; 3:130), cheating (Qur'an 9:34), gambling and games of chance (Qur'an 5:91–2), theft (Qur'an 5:38), and trading in liquor or pork.[3]

However, this right of possession is not absolute, since God is the ultimate owner of all wealth (Qur'an 6:165; 57:7). The concept of viceregency means that the individual is a trustee of his or her property. The right to use and benefit from one's property must not be exercised at the expense of the interest of the community (*ummah*), or otherwise contrary to the Shari'a. In particular, the *ummah*, through its rulers and representatives, has the right to organize the economic system within which wealth is used, and to limit the acquisition of wealth if it contradicts the interest of society at large.

It follows that Islam also envisages a fair amount of 'economic planning', and even public ownership. More will be said about the economic policies of Islamic governments in Chapter 3. We will also defer discussion of Islamic taxation and inheritance law to that chapter. There are some distinctly Keynesian measures contained in the Shari'a for the redistribution of income *and* capital among the population.

3. *Rububiyyah*, meaning God's arrangements for the nourishment and direction of things toward a perfect state. One should note that this concept flatly contradicts the basic tenet of neoclassical economic theory, that goods are in short supply. There is sufficient sustenance for everything and everybody to achieve God's perfect plan for the Universe.

4. *Tazkiyah*, meaning growth and purification. It will be seen that this concept is highly important for Islamic economic theory. Firstly it endorses the ideas of change and expansion, and so avoids the dilemma of canon law, which had no provision for growth and change. Also it means that Islam is not an ascetic faith: people are expected to do their best to obtain a better material life. *However*, all growth, and change, and material enhancement must lead to social justice and spiritual betterment for the *ummah*, as well as the proprietor.

5. *Accountability*, in the sense that everyone is accountable for his or her actions, or inactions, on the Day of Judgement, and the implications of this for life in this world and the next. This is the aspect of Islamic economic policy which most

clearly differentiates it from its non-Islamic counterparts. People cannot behave irresponsibly with the goods, equipment, land and talents entrusted to them, because they will be held to account for them. Moreover, responsibility is interpreted very widely; one must accept all the duties and liabilities of one's possessions, as well as the benefits of ownership.

The business applications of these concepts are entirely practical. Most of the abuses of wealth which come under the heading of 'unfair trading' (which is the strict meaning of 'usury' (*riba*)) arise from the ability of the wealthy to exercise improper pressure, so as to retain the benefits of their wealth, while avoiding the duties and losses attached to its ownership. Many of these practices are entirely acceptable in non-Muslim societies, provided they are not 'excessive'. A typical example would be the receipt and payment of interest on loans. This is absolutely forbidden in Islam, which simply does not accept the concept of 'the time-value of money'. Money is only valuable to the extent that the owner has a use for it; if one can find no immediate, profitable employment for one's capital, it should be loaned without interest. If a profitable investment can be found, the capitalist must take an appropriate share of the risk of loss. A fixed rate of interest over time can only be extortionate (Maududi, 1960; Siddiqui, 1981); it shifts the whole of the risk of loss in its use from the lender to the borrower (Hameedullah, 1970).

More extreme examples are to be found among the practices known as 'off-balance-sheet financing'. A typical scheme of this sort was reported in *Accountancy Age*, on 16 April 1987:

> The Burton Group last year sold £100 million worth of its properties to a company called Hall and Sons through a 'diamond' arrangement in which the shares in the company were divided equally between a 100% subsidiary and a 50% associate. Burtons kept Hall outside its group for Revenue tax purposes but within it for capital gains.
>
> Burtons took a minority of the seats on the board to reflect its 50% direct voting control through the 100% subsidiary. But by its arrangement with the ANZ bank, which provided £70 million non-recourse finance to Hall, the Burton Group has the option to reacquire the properties at cost whenever it likes.
>
> 'We've retained the reward without the risk of ownership,' said Burton Group Treasurer Nigel Robson.

For practical purposes, the Burton Group remains the owner of its properties, but it has managed to substitute them with liquid assets on its balance sheet, while leaving the properties, and the loan secured upon them, 'off-balance-sheet'. The view of the accounting profession has usually been that substance should have precedence over form in such cases. The legal profession disagrees, to the extent of stating that it would advise a client to take action against any auditor who qualified an auditors' report on those grounds. The authors would tend to support the lawyers in this. If it is *'lawful'* to deal with the title to land in this fashion, it is appropriate to account for it in accordance with the legal form, and merely refer to the surrounding rights and liabilities by way of a note. The real question is whether British law itself is *morally* right to permit the formation of organizations whose objectives include schemes to 'retain the reward without the risk of ownership'.

Islamic Forms of Business Organization

Islam, by contrast, has always insisted upon close personal responsibility among the members of a trading organization. In Islam, an organization is considered to be a contract by which two or more individuals agree to contribute either capital or labour to a common undertaking. Any profits or losses accruing to the undertaking are to be distributed among the partners (Al-Kayyat, 1983). A good number of different types of trading company are known to Islamic jurisprudence (*fiqh*), but they are all a form of partnership, rather than true corporate entities. The most common forms are:

1. *Companies based on delegation.* In these companies, each partner delegates to the other partner(s) the right to act as his or her agent, both in his or her absence, or presence. Partners have equal voting rights, and contribute capital and share profits and losses equally. Generally, they have an equal liability for the debts of the company, but some jurists differ on this point.
2. *Companies based on guarantee.* In this case, two or more partners participate in trade, but they may not always contribute the capital in equal shares. Profits are distributed in proportions agreed by the partners, which need not be the same as those in which they have contributed the capital. However, losses are always distributed in the ratio of their respective capital contributions. Again, the operational basis of the company is the mutual agency of all the partners.
3. *Companies based on labour.* These companies are formed where two or more people agree to participate in a business which involves no joint investment of capital. Typically, these will be professional practices, between doctors, lawyers, accountants and so on. Profits are distributed by agreement between the partners.
4. *Companies based on reputation.* Here, the partners do not provide any capital. Instead, they rely on their good reputation to obtain goods on credit, and sell them for cash. Profits are shared out as agreed between the partners. These 'companies' are usually by way of 'joint ventures', with a limited life. Not all Islamic jurists agree on the propriety of such arrangements, although the partners

will remain liable to meet the company's debts in full when payment has to be made.

5. *Companies based upon mudaraba.* These companies consist of two or more partners, where some provide the capital, and the others participate through their labour, or experience and contacts. The sharing of profits is agreed upon in advance, but any losses are borne initially by those partners who have provided the capital, but only to the limit of the capital which they have provided. Although, as we shall see, this is the most common arrangement by which Islamic banks provide money to their customers, its validity as a form of company is not recognized by all Islamic jurists.

These companies are all of the partnership type, and involve a form of agency, which assumes that all the partners will take some part in the management of the enterprise. It might be noted that shares of profit must always be by way of a percentage, and never a lump sum. In the event of insolvency, each partner is jointly and severally liable to make good the whole of the debts of the company, except, of course, in the case of *mudaraba* companies. Joint stock companies, with independent legal entities and limited liability, have not been recognized by Islamic jurists, at least in the past:

> The history of Islamic *fiqh* has not identified the firm as a legal entity whose obligations are separate from its owners, nor has it ever recognized that the firm has a separate financial obligation. (Abdullah, 1983, p. 222)

Nevertheless, corporations with separate legal entities are not unknown in Islamic law, so some jurists see no objection to the extension of this status to trading concerns, if the arrangements conform to the requirements of the Shari'a in other respects:

> [Muslim] jurists did not treat a company as an entity, but they consider a mosque, the state, and an endowment as independent financial entities. It is my view that a company can have such an entity, as is the case of a mosque. (Al-Kayyat, 1958, p. 339)

There is no consensus among Muslim jurists on the issue of limited liability, in particular where none of the participants would have unlimited liability for the whole of the company's debt. Some claim that every business corporation is tantamount to a *mudaraba* company, where the liability of the owners is limited to the amount of their investment (Al-Kafeef, 1962; Al-Kayyat, 1983). This is something of a minority view, since only one of the four main schools of Islamic *fiqh* (the Hanabelites) accepts the *mudaraba* type of company. However, there may be more general agreement that on certain occasions the formation of a particular corporation may benefit the public interest. Then, perhaps, the general prohibition on limited liability should be relaxed in order to assist in its formation (Abdullah, 1986).

Islamic Forms of Lending

As has been said, Islam totally rejects *riba*, by which is meant the receipt and payment of interest. 'But God hath permitted trade and forbidden usury' (Qur'an 2: 275). This means that an Islamic business cannot deal in any negotiable instruments that would entail the receipt or payment of interest. This includes both notes payable and receivable, as well as bonds and debentures, and precludes the capital structure of an Islamic company from having any gearing, or any debt bearing fixed interest. Preference shares are also forbidden, both by reason of the fixed dividend and because the dividend, and often the capital, are repayable in priority to the other shares. The latter grounds, which contravene Islamic ideas of unilateral risk-bearing, prohibit the issuing of founders' shares with rights over and above those of the other shareholders (Al-Kayyat, 1983). Another Western practice which is said to be rejected under Islam is the issuing of securities at a discount. To the extent that the securities were redeemable at or above par at a fixed future date, this 'deep discounting' would constitute a hidden interest payment. However, the issuing of ordinary shares at a discount on their original par value would seem no more than a recognition of the market value of the securities.

Obviously, the prohibition of interest applies to all loans, whether or not they are secured by notes or debentures. A number of alternative financing mechanisms are used by Islamic banks in their dealings with their customers:

1. *Mudaraba*. This is basically a partnership agreement without any specific limit as to its duration, made between the supplier of capital and the entrepreneur (Kahf, 1978). Under this arrangement, lenders supply capital to borrowers as their agents (*mudarib*) for trading purposes, while the borrower, like other agents, contributes only labour and experience. Profits are divided between the parties in some ratio specified in the original agreement. Losses are borne by the lenders to the limit of the capital originally introduced, and the borrowers then receive no reward for their efforts.

2. *Musharaka*. This is a partnership of limited duration, and formed to carry out some specific project. As such, it is much along the lines of the Western joint

venture, or consortium arrangement. Both parties agree to contribute fixed and working capital, and technical and managerial expertise in some proportions, and agree in advance on the division of any profits. Losses are always shared in proportion to the capital contributions.

3. *Murabaha.* This is a mechanism whereby the banks finance the purchase of specific commodities for a fixed cost, plus a negotiated margin of profit. The bank either buys the goods and resells them to the customer, or procures them on his or her behalf. The latter is known as *murabaha*—sales by order of customer. One of the conditions of this type of financing is that both parties should be aware of the original purchase price, as well as the margin of profit. Furthermore, the bank actually has to procure the goods before charging them to the customer. Obviously there can be no relationship between the margin of profit charged by the bank and the length of the credit allowed to the customer. However, it may be agreed that the payment can be made by instalments; in that case the charge will be higher, to cover handling costs.

4. *Ijara.* This is the well-known capital leasing arrangement, whereby a financial house procures an asset and makes it available to its customer on a rental basis. Of course, such contracts are often framed (in the West) as a classic form of 'off-balance-sheet financing'. It must be appreciated that none of these Islamic financial instruments is automatically acceptable (*halal*) under the Shari'a. The terms of each contract need to be considered in detail, to ensure that no usurious terms have been introduced. In this case, any clauses which do not reflect the true substance of a commercial lease, whereby the lessee is using the agreement as a means of acquiring substantially the whole of the risks and/or rewards of ownership, would make it invalid. Most Islamic banks operate Religious Supervisory Boards, whose semi-independent members approve loans and other instruments for these purposes (Briston and El-Ashker, 1987).

5. *Ijara wa iktina.* If the customers do want to borrow money over a long period, so as to acquire a capital asset, they must use what is effectively a formal hire-purchase agreement. The Islamic version involves the bank in procuring the assets, while the customer is given an option on acquiring them by paying agreed instalments into an investment account held by the bank. The bank invests these funds for the customer, in the ordinary way, until the accumulated funds equal the asset price.

6. *Quard hassan.* This is what is known as a 'benevolent loan', and does not involve any charges or interest. Islamic banks provide this service for customers who are facing difficulties, or unexpected expenditures.

In this way, Islamic finance houses are enabled to cover the whole range of their customers' requirements for financial assistance. Obviously, the ratio of profit-sharing, or the amount of the fixed charge, is changed from time to time, for new contracts, and plays much the same role in Islamic banking policy as the interest rates charged by Western-style banks. Equally obviously, the need to observe the Shari'a means that some forms of business transactions which are acceptable in the West cannot be undertaken by Muslims. In general, Islam imposes a style of 'plain dealing' both in investment and in borrowing. *Prima facie* this suggests a Jeffersonian world of rather small, local, personally managed family businesses. Chapter 4 will discuss how far it may be possible to apply these methods to modern, very large-scale international enterprises.

Notes

1. Quoted from Al-Buraey (1985, pp. 148–9).
2. Quoted from Arif (1985, p. 83).
3. See the *Hadith* (saying) of the Prophet Mohammed reported in Al-Bukhari (1951, Vol. 3, p. 74).

Bibliography

Abdullah, M. A. *Al-Shaqseaa al-Ietbariah fi al-Figh al-Islam: Dirasaa Moqarana* (The Legal Entity in Islamic Jurisprudence: A Comparative Study), (Khartoum: Al-Dar Al-Sudania Lilkutb, 1986).

Allen, C. K., *Law and Orders* (London: Stevens, 1965).

Arif, Muhammad, 'Toward the Shari'ah Paradigm of Islamic Economics: The Beginning of a Scientific Revolution', *The American Journal of Islamic Social Sciences*, Vol. 2 No. 1 (1985), pp. 79–99.

Audah, Abd al-Qadir, *Al-Mal Walhukm fi al-Islam* (Money and Government in Islam), 5th edition (Cairo: Al-Muktaar al-Islami, 1977).

Bakhash, Saul, 'Islam and Power Politics', *New York Review of Books*, (21 July 1988), pp. 30–2.

Briston, R., and A. A. El-Ashker, 'Religious Audit: Could It Happen Here?', *The Arab Certified Accountant*, Vol. 1 (February 1987), pp. 53–5.

Al-Bukhari, A. M. Ibn Ismail, *Sahih Al-Bukhari*, (Cairo: Dar Ihyaa al-Kutb al-Arabia (Isa al-Baabi al-Halabi Wa-Shurakaaho), 1951).

Al-Buraey, Muhammed, *Administrative Development: An Islamic Perspective* (London: KPI Ltd, 1985).

Davis, Kenneth, C., *Discretionary Justice* (Urbana, Ill.: University of Illinois, 1971).

Al-Faruqi, Isma'il R., *Islam* (Niles, Ill.: Argus Communications, 1979).

Green, R. W. (Ed.), *Protestantism and Capitalism: The Weber Thesis and Its Critics*, (Boston: 1959).

Hameedullah, M., 'The Economic System of Islam', *in Introduction to Islam* (IIFSO, 1970), pp. 140–68.

Ismael, T. I., and J. S. Ismael, *Government and Politics in Islam* (London: Frances Pinter, 1985).

Al-Kafeef, A., *Al-Sharikat fi al-Fiqh al-Islami* (Companies in Islamic Jurisprudence), (Cairo: Arab Countries League, Institute of Higher Arabic Studies, 1962).

Kahf, Monzer, *The Islamic Economy: Analytical Study of the Functioning of the Islamic*

Economic System (Plainfield, Ind.: Muslim Students' Association of the United States and Canada, 1978).

Al-Kayyat, Abdul-Aziz Izzat, *Al-Sharikat fi al-Shari'a al-Islamia Walganoon al-Wadie* (Companies in the Islamic Shari'a and Company Law), *Part II*, 2nd edition (Beirut: Moaar al-Risalah, 1983).

Maududi, Abdul A'la, *Sud* (Interest), (Lahore: Islamic Publications, 1960).

Qutb, Sayyid, *Al-Adalah al-Ijtim'iyah fi al-Islam* (Social Justice in Islam), (Cairo: 1953).

Sen, A. K., 'Rational Fools: A Critique of the Behavioural Foundations of Economic Theory', *Philosophy and Public Affairs*, Vol. 6 (1976–7), pp. 317–44.

Siddiqui, M. N., *Muslim Economic Thinking: A Survey of Contemporary Literature* (London: The Islamic Foundation, 1981).

Tawney, R. H., *Religion and the Rise of Capitalism: An Historical Study* (London: Murray, 1926).

Umarah, Muhammah, *Al-Khilafa wa Nashaat al-Ahzab al-Islamiyah* (Succession and the Rise of Islamic Parties), (Beirut: al-Mosasah al-Arabiya lil-Dirasat wa al-Nasher, 1977).

Weber, M., 'Die Protestantische Ethik und der Geist des Kapitalismus' (The Protestant Ethic and the Spirit of Capitalism), *Arckiv fur Sozialwissenschaft und Sozialpolitik*, Vols XX and XXI (1904–5).

Appendix to Chapter 2

The Revival of Islam and Modern Business Activity

A Résumé of the Historical Development of the Muslim World

At the present time, the Islamic world seems politically fragmented and economically underdeveloped, except as an oil producer. However, this was not the case at the time of the European Middle Ages, when the foundations of Western capitalism were being laid. Then, those parts of the world under Muslim domination were major centres of military and economic power, and great cultural and scientific excellence. This appendix examines the subsequent history of the Middle East region in search of possible reasons why modern large-scale industry has not developed in those countries. Some analysts, such as Tawney, have supposed that Islam itself prevented this:

> The way in which the Muslim religion seems most often to have influenced in a negative manner the evolution of the economy in a capitalist direction is through the ban on lending at interest and on aleatory contracts. (Tawney, 1926, p. 138)

This seems unlikely, given the wholehearted endorsement of trade and self-betterment referred to in the main body of this chapter.

Other analysts, including Marx and Weber, have suggested that the essential basis for the growth of full-blown capitalism is the development of assured property rights, supported by a legal system which is independent of the whims and interests of local rulers. In Europe, canon law did at least provide the concept of rights and duties of an absolute kind, with a supranational authority to enforce them. The Protestant ideal of the Christian calling reinforced the concept of private property rights still further. The

41

latter part of the main body of this chapter demonstrates that Islam is equally supportive of the rule of law and private property. Nevertheless, it may be that the *political* climate of the Middle East created an ideology which was inimical to the creation of an independent judiciary and secure property-owning, despite an outward conformity to Islam.

This ideology (it is argued) was the product of the basic instability which dogged the Ottoman Empire throughout its long history. Islam was revealed at Mecca and Medina, in the Arabian Peninsula, at the beginning of the seventh century of the Christian era. The major powers in the region which largely coincides with the present-day Muslim world were the Byzantine and the Persian Empires. These empires had been embroiled in a conflict for supremacy which left them both in a severely weakened state. As a result, the followers of Islam were able to establish control over a large part of the region. Initially, this was a single, if loose, federation of tribal chieftains, owing allegiance to the Prophet and his successors. As was described in the main body of the chapter, disputes over the legitimacy of these successors led to the break-up of the unified Muslim federation. Even so, it seems probable that the political disunity in the Muslim world was no worse than that of contemporary Europe.

The impossibility of finding a generally acceptable religious leader in a movement which placed considerable emphasis on political and social unity, created a power vacuum which was filled by what eventually became the Ottoman Empire (1252–1914), with its centre at what was formerly Constantinople, the capital city of the Byzantine Empire. Since the original Muslim militia was hopelessly divided on matters of succession, a substantial element of the Ottoman military and civil government consisted of cadres of non-Muslims. The Circassians, Serbians and other minority peoples recruited for this purpose were nominally slaves, but their duties as soldiers and civil servants meant that they were very influential. Thus, while nominally Muslim, the Ottoman Empire probably lacked the commitment of a true Islamic State. Moreover, Muslim and non-Muslim soldiers alike were also a grave danger to the State; like European governments of the time, the Ottoman Empire was always in difficulties over meeting their pay. This problem was overcome by the expedient of giving senior officers tax-gathering and general landlord-style rights over stretches of territory. Their tenure was theoretically limited, and also liable to revocation by the local bey or his superiors.

The division in Islam had caused another problem. Islam was no longer producing laws. Although the principles laid down by the Prophet are held to be immutable, the main body of the chapter has shown how individual

Muslims have always had the power of *ijtihad*. Nowadays, as has been said, this is simply a right of discussion and persuasion, leading to normal legislative action. However, the period between the Prophet's death and the break-up of the federation is known as 'the '*Ijtihad* Period', when the *ulama* met together and hammered out suitable laws to deal with new situations which faced Islam. When this could no longer be done, the *ulama* was reduced to its present honourable, but advisory status.

Faced with the need to administer some sort of justice in the territories, the Ottomans instituted a system of *cadis* (judges). These people never enjoyed a great reputation among those over whom they had jurisdiction. They were, correctly, supposed to be subservient to the local bey, who appointed them. The effect has been that, for much of its history, the Islamic world has had a dual system of law. The official one was largely secular, but also capricious and unprogressive. As against this, there has been the *ulama*, who have kept the Shari'a alive and (to some extent) up to date. However, its influence has been largely domestic, and occasionally, as we shall see, revolutionary.

The Ottoman political and administrative machinery is often said to have combined with Islamic ideas of predestination to produce a profoundly fatalistic ideology. This, the argument continues, made Muslims unwilling to commit resources to long-term investment of any kind. If God willed it to be done, it *would* be done; moreover, the bey and the cadi might always decide to take away one's property, or even one's life. The result was what was called 'the oriental mode of production': a world of small traders, peasants and workers, with an administrative aristocracy, which nevertheless lacked the territorial security of the feudal system.

A further alternative analysis is that of Maxime Rodinson, who argues (1977) that Muslim faith and Muslim ideology had little influence on the economic life of Islam's adherents, either before or after the emergence of capitalism in the West. In particular, his view is that the Muslim religion has not had any significant influence on either the structure or the functioning of the capitalist sector in Islamic countries (p. 168). Adopting a Marxian analysis, Rodinson claims that the commercial and financial activities (which is what he defines as the capitalistic sector) to be found in the Muslim world of the Middle Ages were very similar to those of medieval Europe.

Rodinson believes that the practice of the traditional Muslim world, broadly speaking, was not unfaithful to the theoretical precepts of the Qur'an (Rodinson, 1977, p. 74). These favourable conditions continued for a considerable period of time:

Not only did the Muslim world know a capitalistic sector, but this sector was apparently the most extensive and highly developed in history, before the establishment of the world market created by the Western bourgeoisie, and this did not outstrip it in importance until the sixteenth century. The extent of the market was simply due to the military victories of Islam, the long duration of the unified Muslim Empire, and the power of the ideological bond that prevented watertight frontiers from being formed between the different parts when it did eventually break up. (Rodinson, 1977, pp. 56–7)

Since the same prototypical capitalistic sector existed in both worlds, Islam itself cannot have been an obstacle to the initial stages of further evolution towards modern capitalism in the Muslim regions. Rodinson discounts the significance of the Islamic prohibition of interest payments. Since the Shari'a and Christian canon law have identical views on usury,

[T]here is nothing to indicate in a compelling way that the Muslim religion prevented the Muslim world from developing along the road to modern capitalism, any more than that Christianity directed the Western European world along that road. (Rodinson, 1977, p. 117)

Rodinson concludes that since the causes of the divergence cannot be found in men's adherence to some pre-established doctrine, modern capitalism must result from an independent growth of secularism in medieval and later Europe which did not find any counterpart in the East. This view could find further support in the fact that when large-scale capitalism came to the Muslim world, it was as part of a general movement toward formal secularization in the nineteenth century. This came about as a result of the final decline and fragmentation of the Ottoman Empire, and the concomitant expansion of the influence of the European powers in the Middle East (Al-Buraey, 1985; Ismael and Ismael, 1985). Its immediate source was the impact of European colonization and 'commercial imperialism'. However, there were many people living in those areas who felt the allure of European civilization and Western technology, quite independently. Their attempts to imitate the alien culture involved their acceptance of its underlying philosophy of separating temporal and spiritual aspects of life. This process of secularization reached its climax in the aftermath of the First World War.

Secularism in Islamic Countries

The road to secularism pursued by the heartland of the old Ottoman Empire, modern Turkey, was characterized by the abolition of the Islamic framework of government supplied by the *khilafa* (see the main body of the chapter). In addition, the Shari'a code was replaced by secular commercial law, which permitted, among other things, the use of interest in economic transactions. This was followed (in 1865) by the establishment of a Western-style banking system, operating on the basis of interest-bearing loans and deposits. This adoption of European codes of political and commercial philosophy took place despite the fact that the ownership and personnel of organizations involved were often entirely Muslim. This trend has continued: most Muslim and Western scholars agree that most, if not all, Muslim countries today are following their ex-colonial masters' model in their quest for economic development (Sardar, 1979).

Ismael and Ismael (1985, p. 36) specify three basic positions that were assumed by those advocating the Westernization of their countries' institutions:

1. *Westernization for its own sake*, whereby advancement was sought through copying the social, political, economic and technological institutions and structures of the West.
2. *Liberalism*, which implied that people's minds should be freed from the bondage of preconceived beliefs and traditions, in order to examine empirically, and in complete independence, all the issues relevant to knowledge and society.
3. *Secularism for its own sake*, which called for a constitution based upon civil law, and the establishment of a state on 'modern Western foundations', where religion and government would be separated.

However, this tide of secularism did not flow unopposed. The development of such secular ideas continually provoked the opposition of those Muslims who believed sincerely that the separation of religious and temporal affairs should not exist. These groups often called for an even stricter return to the fundamental teachings of Islam, as specified by the Shari'a, in all aspects of life, political, economic and social. Prominent leaders of such counter-reformation movements were Jamal al-Din al-Afgani (1893–6) in Iran; Muhammad Abduh (1849–1905) and Hassn al-Banna (1906–49) in Egypt; Rashid Redha (1865–1935) in Tripoli; Abd al-Rahman al-Bazzaz (1913–73) in Morocco; Abul ala-Mawdoudi in Pakistan; and Muhammed Ahmed al-Mahdi (1848–85) in Sudan.

Although they all had the complete Islamicization of their country's institutions as their objective, these scholars pursued it in very different ways. Some sought to mobilize Muslims through a group or party, like the Jamiyat al-Urwa al-Wathqa in Iran, the Jama'ati Islami in Pakistan, and the Ikhwan (Muslim Brotherhood) in Egypt. The last-named group has been particularly influential outside Egypt; it operates in most countries of the Middle East, and a number of fundamentalist groups are generally supposed to be offshoots from it. These groups have been equally various in their methods. Some have sought to penetrate the existing system from within, others to integrate with and so influence the ruling party. Again, others have simply withdrawn from a secular society, like the Iranian religious leaders before the Revolution of 1979; still others have engaged in open opposition, like the Muslim Brotherhood in Egypt and Syria. Finally, there are a few cases in which these groups have started an open insurrection against a secular state: the Mahdist Revolution in Sudan (1881–98), and the Iranian Revolution of 1979.

These continuous efforts by the counter-reformers enjoyed comparatively little success until the late 1960s. The strength of secularism is that it is not specifically atheistic, but merely attempts to restrict the sphere of influence of religion. Thus, for example, as early as 1906, the Persian Constitution gave the *ulama* an official role in determining the compatibility of the country's laws with Islam, and rescinding those found to be inconsistent with the Shari'a. Nevertheless, this provision was largely ineffective, because of the Pahlavi Shahs' continuous attempts to counteract its implementation and pursue vigorous policies of Westernization. The situation is now very different in a number of Muslim countries, where very definite moves are being made to create truly Islamic States.

Ismael and Ismael (1985) argue that discontent among the less well-off social classes was a major factor contributing to the success of the Iranian Revolution in 1979, as well as the pro-Western attitude of the government, and foreign intervention in Iranian affairs. This seems likely. Many people in most Muslim countries remain desperately poor, and may have become comparatively much poorer despite over a century of 'Westernization'. The current resurgence of Islam in Muslim countries

[does] not simply reflect the reaffirmation of Muslims in their faith, but rather expresses deep-seated social concerns that are reflected in a situation of a 'society-in-crisis'. (Cudsi and Dessouki, 1981, p. 7)

Since defying the teachings of the Prophet has failed to produce even material betterment for anyone except a small élite, it is unsurprising that these people are prepared to accept an experiment with an Islamic State. As we have seen, Islam promises the faithful happiness and prosperity in this life, as well as in the world to come.

Bibliography

Al-Buraey, Muhammed, *Administrative Development: An Islamic Perspective* (London: KPI Ltd., 1985).

Cudsi, A. S., and Alie Dessouki (Eds.), *Islam and Power* (London: Croom Helm, 1981).

Ismael, T. Y., and J. S. Ismael, *Government and Politics in Islam* (London: Frances Pinter, 1985).

Rodinson, Maxime, *Islam and Capitalism* (London: Penguin Books, 1977).

Sardar, Ziauddin, *The Future of Muslim Civilization* (London: Croom Helm, 1979).

Tawney, R. H., *Religion and the Rise of Capitalism: An Historical Study* (London: Murray, 1986).

Chapter 3

The Financial Policies of the Islamic State

'Church and State'

The basic political principles underlying the government of an Islamic State were described in Chapter 2. These political principles were little different from the economic principles governing the management of the individual's private property. There *is* no distinction to be drawn between 'business', 'public affairs', and even 'private life' in Islam: all are subject to the requirements of the Shari'a. Chapter 2 also related how religious law came to be excluded from business life in Europe in the eighteenth century. The same anti-clerical spirit which brought about this dichotomy was probably even more apparent in the public affairs of Europe and North America at that time. The separation of 'Church' and 'State' underlay much of the political tension of the late eighteenth and early nineteenth centuries. In England, where patriotic loyalty demanded allegiance to the (broad Protestant) Church of England, both (Roman Catholic) recusants and the generally more influential (Calvinistic) dissenters sought an end to the limitations placed on their advancement in many official careers, through the secularization of government, the universities, the judiciary and so on. The Constitution of the United States of America specifically provides for the exclusion of religion from affairs of state.

Neither dichotomy can exist under Islam. However, their absence has other effects besides enhancing the influence of the *ulama* on both business and administrative practice. It means that both government officers and business people are keenly interested in religious matters, perhaps for reasons other than personal piety! This was true in medieval Europe also, where both princes and merchants' guilds often sent emissaries to Rome, seeking guidance (and lobbying for relaxation) over the impact of canon law on their affairs (Tawney, 1926). We have described the institution of Shariʿa committees in Islamic banks at the present time. But there are other implications for life in an Islamic State. Because there is no distinction between public life and private life, it may be that individual Muslims of the humbler kind are less disposed than their non-Muslim counterparts to see government as a matter 'to be left to their betters'. As was described in the Appendix to Chapter 2, it has never been difficult to orchestrate quite general opposition to political changes which were seen to contravene the teachings of Islam. The general requirement for *shura* (consultation) means that Muslim employees should be equally unafraid to speak their minds on matters of business.

The purpose of this chapter is to say something about yet another natural consequence of the essential unity of Islamic life. No one doubts that an Islamic government has not just the power, but a positive duty to intervene in economic affairs. This was apparent from the conduct of public affairs during the Prophet's own lifetime, and under the first four *Khalifas* (successors). The administrative history of those times is of significance, since this was the so-called *Ijtihad* Period, during which the principles of Islam were elucidated. However, it is important to bear in mind that Islam does not imply an unchanging conservatism, in administration or anything else; the institutions themselves were, no doubt, appropriate to their time and no other. Indeed, the actual system of officials and departments of state (*diwans*) does not differ greatly from those to be found in the more advanced parts of medieval Europe. Even the existence of an Auditor-General's Department (*diwan al-azimmah*) 'to control and check the accounts of the other *diwans*, supervise their work, and act as the intermediary between the other *diwans* and the office of vizierate' (Al-Buraey, 1985, p. 260; also Baagir and Awad, 1981) merely indicates that despite the incessant warfare and expansion of the times, the early Islamic federation was unusually well organized from the first. Something will be said of the remaining *diwans* and their activities in the appendix to this chapter.

The Hisbah

However, one administrative unit of the early Islamic State is especially worthy of mention here: this was the *hisbah*. This institution was fully developed under the Abbasids, and played an important role in ensuring that government resources were properly managed according to the Shariʿa.

Hisbah is defined as the promotion of good and the prevention of evil. The Qur'an says:

> Let there arise out of you a band of people inviting to all that is good, enjoining what is right, and forbidding what is wrong; they are the ones to attain felicity. (3:104)

This office was the one specifically charged with maintaining the theocratic nature of Islamic society as a whole, as opposed to mere administrative efficiency of its government departments, which was the province of the *diwan al-azimmah*:

> [The *hisbah*] seeks the penetration of ethical and religious standards into day-to-day affairs, especially business and trade. This is so because *hisbah* is not only an institution of the spiritual order, but also an integral organization of the total Islamic environment, which manifests mundane and material aspects as well. (Al-Buraey, 1985, p. 263)

The title of the person who headed the institution of *hisbah* was *mutasib*, or *sahib al-suq* (market inspector, or supervisor). To qualify for the post, the person should be a free Muslim, of full age and understanding, and someone of sound judgement and energy, and well versed in religious knowledge (Ibn al-Ukhuwwah, 1937). His primary duties in the markets of the day were to prevent the monopoly of goods, and to control the pricing of goods, but only if this was in the public interest and could not be achieved in other ways (Ibn al-Qayyam, 1953). The functions also included seeing that the essential public utilities were well maintained; ensuring that the revenues of the State were collected, especially from those who would evade them; and preventing the unlawful expenditure or waste of State funds (Al-Mawardi, 1978). Presumably the last-named duties supplemented the activities of the *diwan al-azimmah*, and involved the application of the true principles of the Shari'a to those who fell short of their ideals, while still fulfilling the outward 'letter of the law'.

Obviously, the ecclesiastical courts of medieval Europe had a similar function, but it may be that they often lacked such well-organized cadres of officials. It should be noted that *hisbah* did not exist, as such, under the Prophet and the four *Khalifas*. They supervised such matters in person; the Prophet Mohammed was especially active in these matters, possibly because of his extensive experience of business as a younger man. The need for a specific institution was felt after the expansion of the Islamic State made it difficult to cover the vastly increased number of business and administrative transactions. Sadly, the office lost its significance in later years, as the (effectively secular) Ottoman Empire developed. Incompetent officers came to be appointed, and an aura of corruption became general (Al-Mawardi, 1978). This was the point at which the patrimonialism noted in the Appendix to Chapter 2 became a norm of earlier Islamic society.

It might be supposed that an institution like *hisbah* would also be of value in a modern Islamic State. As we have seen in earlier chapters of this book, not a few devices of modern finance involve an outward form that is very different from the underlying substance: these include capital leasing and most other forms of off-balance-sheet finance. Again, ingenious minds devise methods of operating on the stock exchanges and commodity markets, whose overall effect is contrary to the principles of the Shari'a. Dealings in 'futures', trading on indices and the problems of detecting 'insider trading' all are issues which require informed investigation. Questions of monopoly and price-fixing are now more serious and more difficult to control, given the existence of large national and international enterprises.

The institution of *hisbah* might also prove very useful in a variety of moral issues which can arise in corporate reporting. Here again, it is possible to report truthfully about the financial and overt legal implication of a company's activities, while choosing to ignore a variety of spiritual and social problems which are affected by them (Gambling and Karim, 1986). 'Social Accounting', 'Social Audit', and similar concerns such as 'Human Resource Accounting' and 'Energy Accounting' are all attempts to take into account what are known as 'externalities'. These are the difference between the 'social cost' and the 'private cost' of production. Sincere efforts are often made to deal with the issues in the West, but truly satisfactory solutions have yet to emerge. What we said in Chapter 1 about human perceptions and reality suggests why the problem is so difficult to resolve. The 'private costs' are very closely related to the variables in our conscious models of the Universe. The 'social costs' are related to the underlying reality, which we appreciate only unconsciously, through common sense.

It follows that the content of 'social accounting' cannot be verbalized very adequately; it can only be appreciated truly through participation in social rituals. The remaining chapters of the book will have a good deal to say about how an Islamic company ought to keep itself open to the receipt of unspoken, common-sense messages of this kind. It is unlikely that the European business people whose cumulative efforts led to the compartmentalization of religion were unusually degraded specimens of humanity. Expertise tends to reinforce specialization, hence it is probable that most people find it easier to structure their lives so that the common sense messages which they receive require a minimum of reconciliation with their conscious models of their environments. It is likely that Muslim business people feel the same urge 'to keep their eyes on the shop'.

The purpose of revealed religion (and humanistic morality) is to prevent this happening. God (as Muslims see things) does not *need* our belief and worship, but our simple obedience to His instructions. The whole purpose of the Shari'a could be seen as inhibiting Muslims from enclosing their lives so as to exclude messages from either God or any part of creation. Unfair dealing (*riba*), whether by the use of interest calculations in place of common concern for the employment of capital, or otherwise, involves shutting the inward or outward ear to some of these messages. This is where the independence of an office such as *hisbah* may be essential to the proper conduct of business. Everything which is internal to the business entity, to the industry or even to 'the economy' endorses some degree of compartmentalization of interest. There is a need for an organ of the State to ensure 'the penetration of ethical and religious standards into day-to-day affairs', so that our common sense can be truly effective.

Keynesian Aspects of Islamic Law

One very obvious way in which the Shari'a attempts to keep a Muslim's economic life open to the calls of society is through the *zakah* system of taxation, raised to provide for the relief of poverty and other forms of social security. Another is through the Islamic rules of inheritance. We shall see that both reflect a definite 'economic policy', namely a Keynesian concern for the wider distribution of spending power throughout the community. This is because there is a general principle in Islam that wealth should not be monopolized in the hands of a few individuals, since this will create social imbalance (Qur'an 59:7). These requirements constitute basic religious duties for every Muslim, on a par with those enjoining prayer, fasting and pilgrimage. To that extent, Muslims are expected to distribute their wealth in accordance with these rules, irrespective of whether the State itself takes any part in the process of collection and distribution.

Zakah is an annual payment which is obligatory on all Muslims. It is levied on money, and the net realizable value of investments (for income generation), animals, and undertakings of all kinds in agriculture, trade or industry. The wealth which is subject to *zakah* must have these characteristics:

1. It must be the beneficial and rightful property of the taxpayer; thus it excludes *waqf* (endowment or trust property), and wealth of an illegitimate nature.
2. It must have the capacity to grow in value, or otherwise produce further wealth.
3. It must be in excess of the *hisab*, which is the minimum amount of wealth which can attract *zakah*.
4. It must also be in excess of the basic needs of the taxpayer.
5. It must be unencumbered by debt.
6. It must have been held for one whole lunar year.

In part this is a pure wealth tax: all money which is put aside and not used for a whole lunar year has *zakah* of 2½ per cent levied upon it. In some cases it is an income tax: for arable cultivation, the tax is 10 per cent, levied on the produce as soon as it has been harvested, while for manufacturing industry, the rate is 10 per cent on net profit only. Otherwise it is a combined tax on net worth and net profits, at a rate of 2½ per cent. Those eligible to receive benefits from the *Zakah* fund are laid down in the Qur'an (9:60). These include the poor (including *fuqara'* (the Muslim poor) and *masakin* (poor among resident aliens)); those employed to administer the *Zakah* fund; those whose hearts have been reconciled to truth (recent converts—and this heading is also taken to include efforts to convert unbelievers); those who are in bondage (slaves and prisoners of war); those unable to pay their debts; those in the path of Allah (holy men and women, although this is nowadays taken to include the establishment of hospitals and schools, and a wide range of social security schemes, such as low-cost housing for the poor); and wayfarers. It can be seen that these beneficiaries are drawn from a wider range of people than is usual in secular benefit schemes.

In this respect, it should be remembered that the payment of *zakah* is *in addition* to a general requirement for all Muslims to support their close relatives. These include the maintenance of one's spouse and children (males until the age of puberty, and females until marriage), needy parents, grandparents and siblings (Qur'an 4:36). There is also a duty to extend help to more distant kinsfolk, and to needy neighbours (Qur'an 17:26). It can be seen that anyone living in a predominantly Muslim community can expect a fair degree of financial and other support in the event of falling into difficulties. This may explain some other features of Muslim finance. There is a general dislike of the concept of insurance and pension funds, on the ground that they may undermine this very generally felt duty to aid the poor and suffering. They also involve unloading one's own risks onto others, which is suspect. On the other hand, third-party motor insurance is compulsory in most Muslim countries! The duty of relatives and even the *Zakah* fund to help debtors may also support the dislike of limitation of liability.

The Keynesian nature of *zakah* prompts those possessing money to invest or otherwise spend their money. It also gives an incentive to traders to ensure the maximum turnover of their net capital. Given the absence of interest, it can be seen that uninvested money will be entirely eaten up by the tax, over time. Even the wealth of orphans is liable to *zakah*; the Prophet Mohammed himself urged that such funds be invested by their guardians 'so that it will not be eaten up by the *zakah*'. At the same time, Islam encourages Muslims to invest their funds sensibly, and neither gamble them away, nor otherwise waste them (Qur'an 6:141).

Another aspect of Keynesian policy is to secure the widest distribution of wealth, in the belief that a lower marginal utility of money may make the very rich liable to hoard money, or invest it very unprofitably. This objective is also enjoined by the Shari'a through the Islamic system of inheritance. A deceased Muslim's belongings must, for the most part, be distributed in specified shares among his or her relatives, including all surviving children, a surviving spouse, and surviving parents. Under some circumstances, brothers and sisters, and even more remote kinsfolk, may inherit an appropriate share. Only one-third of a Muslim's possessions can be willed away from these heirs, even where the deceased had (in some sense) good grounds for wishing to do so.

As in many Western countries, the law governing this aspect of property is among the most complex sections of the Islamic legal code. The circumstances in which more remote relatives may inherit and the shares they receive are especially difficult, and the area is one where the various schools of *fiqh* differ in some minor respects. Nevertheless, it is clear that no element of primogeniture can exist in Islam; there is no especial place for the eldest son. Combined with the effect of *zakah*, this means that every individual is expected to make his or her fortune by themselves, to a large extent. Obviously, very wealthy families exist in Islamic countries, as elsewhere. However, upon examination they will almost always be seen to be very much 'extended families', whose apparent leaders in any one generation are quite loosely related to their predecessors.

It can be seen that these generally socially-desirable effects could have contributed in some degree to the problems of patrimonialism discussed in the Appendix to Chapter 2. The feudal system could not develop without primogeniture in land-holding. It may be that a more limited distribution of deceased estates might have helped the development of large-scale capitalism in those areas, to the extent that larger resources would be at the personal disposition of single individuals. Of course, as was said in that appendix, neither factor could have much impact, in the absence of a firm system of property-rights.

Islam and Economic Planning

The nature of *zakah* shows that Islam is not a neutral force when it comes to fiscal policy. Turning to more general aspects of economic policy, this suggests that an Islamic State will always be active in some form of 'economic planning'. Islam's concern for personal responsibility for wealth probably militates against the establishment of a complete command economy of the socialist/communist type. However, there are ample precedents for a considerable degree of State ownership. The Shari'a prohibits the control of essential resources such as water, grazing, food and fuel by an individual or group of individuals, since they are considered as communal property[1] (Qutb, 1953). In addition, it is also considered appropriate for the State to enter into joint ventures with firms in the private sector, on the basis of *sharikat* (a cooperative, or consortium). This is useful either where the project is too large for the latter to execute independently, or where it is in too sensitive an area for private development, yet too large for the State to finance without help either from its own private sector, or from overseas.

Nevertheless, there is very little evidence of practical application of Islamic forms of national economic planning. For the reasons set out in the Appendix to Chapter 2, Muslim countries have tended to suffer from economic underdevelopment. This is true even of the 'oil-rich' countries in the Gulf and elsewhere. Their wealth comes almost exclusively from the extraction and sale of an exhaustible natural resource, and they rely for the most part on imports from other, usually better developed countries for the necessities of life.

As a result, such economic planning as has been applied has also been an import, arising as an incident in a 'package' of foreign aid. The content of the package has been much the same whether the aid has come from Western capitalist countries or Eastern-bloc communist ones. Both conduct their own economies according to philosophies which agree on one point, at least: prosperity is equated with the accumulation of capital goods, whether by the individual or by the State. As a result, the problems of underdevelopment are seen as proceeding from a 'gap' in capital formation, which needs to be filled by foreign aid (Ahmad, 1979).

The emphasis of *continuous* capital growth seems to promote considerable economic instability, wherever it is used as the basis of economic policy, because the demand for capital goods and the demand for consumer goods and services are not always complementary. Already prosperous countries may be able to absorb fluctuations of this kind, to some extent, but the policy is more problematic in underdeveloped countries, which become enmeshed in a descending spiral of debt. The objective of Islamic economic planning cannot be anything as simple-minded as 'catching up with the West'—or with the East for that matter. This has been amply demonstrated by the unhappy history of most Muslim countries over the last century (see the Appendix to Chapter 2). Their emphasis on capital formation is suspect, since Islam's concern is for Man, rather than equipment for its own sake. The main text of Chapter 2 shows that the idea of growth itself is not at all contrary to the teachings of Islam. These look forward to a continuous improvement in Man's estate, in this world as well as in the next.

It will be remembered that the Arabic word for this principle of growth was *tazkiyah*, with a meaning which combines economic growth with personal purification. This might suggest a programme of development which was no more than a matter of platitude: an emphasis on the development of the human resources of a country, through investment in education, and in improving 'the quality of life' of its inhabitants. These are the ideals of liberal thinkers everywhere, but 'successful' economic policies (in the sense of 'those which get put into effect') invariably pursue purely material ends. It may be that the Islamic insistence on the holistic nature of policy could overcome this apparent weakness in such policies. Social development cannot be divorced from economic development, any more than the latter can be separated from political and religious development. 'Education' and 'quality of life' are empty phrases when divorced from the economic activity which both requires them, and makes them possible.

A Muslim country might determine that it would not be content to supply, or manufacture, whatever seemed most in demand, or easiest to supply, whether for home consumption, or for export. Not only might the country decline to deal in alcohol, or articles made from pigs (because they are not *halal*), but it could choose to concentrate its efforts on producing socially useful items, as opposed to luxury goods. A similar approach could be adopted to methods of production; often foreign aid is given on terms which force recipients to purchase capital equipment from the highly developed donors. Many modern machine-tools require only a few, highly skilled operatives. This may be a sensible idea in the countries where they are produced, but it can be counter-productive if the tools are installed in places where high unemployment goes with low levels of technical skill. Highly

56

specialized equipment may not always produce the optimal results, even where operatives can be found; it can inhibit the application of common sense. Such machine-tools are highly inflexible as to what they can produce and the rate at which they will operate, and modern production-engineering methods have demonstrated that this can lead to the need to hold excessive inventories, and failure to detect wasteful methods and faulty production (Schonberger, 1986).

A policy of not seeking the easiest modes of operation could suggest more controversial policies. The basic problem of underdevelopment is an over-reliance on the sale of raw materials and agricultural products, with manu-facturing industry being largely confined to assembling components made elsewhere. Attempts to correct these problems through protection of local industry by tariffs tends to produce retaliation from other countries. More-over, there is evidence that such protective policies can promote inefficiency among those benefited by the tariffs. It might be that Islamic emphasis on hard work, fair wages and fair prices would prevent inefficiency even where such policies could be practised without disaster, but the matter of retalia-tion is more difficult. One solution might be for Muslim countries to reduce their economic dependence upon both capitalist and socialist countries outside Islam.

Even economic isolationism is undesirable if the policy is pursued in the spirit of the like-minded 'sticking together' for mutual benefit. In any case, the effect would be no more than that of a discriminatory tariff. However, it would be justified to the extent that all Islamic States were following a policy of *tazkiyah*; the different priorities applying under the economizing policies elsewhere must make anything but quite marginal interdependence a likely source of misunderstanding and actual harm.

Economic Regulation in the Islamic State

Economic planning is not confined to policy-making, in any case; the Islamic State must also consider how to secure compliance with its plan, even among its own citizens. There can be no dispute as to the right of Islamic States to intervene directly in the economic lives of its people. A system for licensing what should be made, where and how it should be made, and what should and should not be imported and exported should be the norm in such a society. On the other hand, it is well known that the granting and withholding of licences of this sort commonly breeds corrup-tion, and history suggests that Muslim countries have not been immune from this disease. This again reminds us of the Utopian nature of the Islamic State; if it is not true that to be a good Muslim is the natural condition of every human being, an Islamic State would no better than any other—and perhaps operating under a greater burden of hypocrisy than most. The Appendix to Chapter 2 argues that history has never yet given Islam the opportunity to show what it can do under conditions of peace and stability. Given the opportunity of living in a state where everything is directed toward encouraging and rewarding the good and discouraging and punishing the bad, a Muslim should be expected to have a total commitment to the good.

Given such a level of commitment, one might wonder whether any regulatory machinery would be required in the first place. This argument might be especially appealing when the issues involved are of a highly technical nature—as they commonly are in matters of economics and finance. It might seem that self-regulation is the only hope of applying control in a continually developing situation, where those who are not in day-to-day contact with the field must necessarily be 'out of date'. Examples of the contrasting approaches can be found far removed from Islam: American stock exchanges are subject to a government agency (the Securities and Exchanges Commission), while the British markets are self-regulated by the Council of the Stock Exchange. The American record for detecting *major* frauds (in advance of financial disaster) has not been noticeably better than that of the British.

However, this fact only emphasizes an issue which is central to what this book is saying about both accounting and finance in general. Accounting and finance are neutral methodologies which take on the moral colouring of the backgrounds against which they operate. A Muslim should ask whether it is right that courses of dealings should be so involved, and so far removed from common experience, that only insider 'experts' can begin to assess their moral implications. The State has an interest in the running of these markets, because the community at large (the *ummah*) has an interest in the stability of all markets; it seems essential that the markets should operate in such a way that external regulation remains feasible. Chapters 2 and 4 argue that the Shari'a actually forbids over-elaborate vehicles of investment, on the grounds that they debilitate the personal responsibility of investors for what is being done with the resources committed to their care under God. Sophisticated patterns of dealing on the capital markets often reflect the undesirable nature of the securities—and the devious behaviour of those dealing in them.

Moreover, the possibility of creating financial chaos through the improper expansion of credit leads on to the need for controlling credit, and the supply of money in all its forms. The traditional Western methods of control are through manipulation of the base-rate of interest, and the sale of comparatively short-dated government loans. The prohibition of *riba* prevents the direct application of the same methods in Islam. However, Islamic loans involve an agreed share of profit going to the lender, and it has been suggested that varying the share of profit would have much the same effect as varying a rate of interest. Presumably an Islamic national bank would adjust its share of such profits, and have the same knock-on effect to other loans as a change of base-rate does in the West.

The Islamic view of market operations involving government bonds is more complex. An interesting proposal is that an Islamic government could be said to have an income, in the form of those taxes it can raise which are not allocated to a specific object (see the appendix to this chapter). Maybe it would be appropriate to issue bonds which entitled holders to a fixed percentage of the country's future unallocated revenues, as opposed to a fixed rate of interest on the sum advanced to its government (Anwar, 1987).

Finally, any system of national economic planning requires information to be returned to the appropriate planning agencies by local authorities, financial institutions, and at least the larger industrial and commercial enterprises of the country. The appendix to this chapter shows that such a system existed in the early Islamic State in a fairly well-developed form. As has been discussed in Chapter 1, the inevitable unreliability of such statistics, especially at the national level (Morgenstern, 1964), is no argument against their preparation and use, as a necessary part of the on-going common sense by which human affairs must develop.

Those countries which practise fairly rigorous forms of national economic planning commonly require enterprises operating within their borders to conform to some standardized accounting procedures (e.g. Most, 1984). This is likely to be especially desirable in Islamic countries, for reasons to be developed in the concluding chapters of this book. We shall argue that Islamic businesses may have less *internal* need for formal accounting records than their Western or Soviet counterparts. In general, this is because an Islamic manager must always 'manage by walking about', if only to secure the involvement of his employees, however humble, in the processes of the enterprise. This does not imply that the Islamic company will keep fewer records for that reason alone; indeed, we shall argue that it might properly keep records about matters which are not often so formally kept in the West. Nevertheless, it would follow that such records will find their principal uses as raw materials for official returns to government agencies, and for that reason should be in a standard format.

Such an approach makes sense in an Islamic context. The State is the outward vehicle of the *ummah*, the community of the faithful. Although the conduct of a business is the undivided personal responsibility of those to whom it belongs, they own it as vice-regents, or trustees. The beneficiaries of the trust are the *ummah*, who therefore have the right to know what is going on, and to devise and adjust the rules which govern the conduct of the business.

Notes

1. See the *Hadith* of the Prophet Mohammed reported in the Ibn Majah (1954) and Abu Dawud (undated).

Bibliography

Abu Dawud Salaiman Ibn al-Ash'ath, *Sunan* (Beirut: Dar al-Fikr, undated).

Ahmad, K., 'Economic Development in an Islamic Framework', *in* K. Ahmad and Z. I. Ansari (Eds.), *Islamic Perspectives: Studies in Honour of Sayyid Abdul A'la Mawdudi* (London: The Islamic Foundation, 1979), pp. 223–40.

Anwar, M., *Modelling Interest-Free Economy: A Study of Macro-economics and Development* (International Institute of Islamic Thought, 1987).

Baagir, M. S., and N. M. Awad, 'Diwan al-Azzimah/Diwan al-Ragabaah al-Maleeah Min al-Fikr al-Muhaasabe al-Arabi al-Islami', *Zanko: Section B, Humanities*, Vol. 7 No. 2 (1981), pp. 5–34.

Al-Buraey, Muhammad, *Administrative Development: An Islamic Perspective* (London: KPI Ltd., 1985).

Gambling, T. E., and R. A. A. Karim, 'Islam and Social Accounting', *Journal of Business Finance and Accounting*, Vol. 13 (1986), pp. 39–50.

Ibn al-Qayyam al-Jouzeyah, *Al-Torog al-Hikmeyah fi al-Siyasa al-Shar'eeyah* (Cairo: Al-Sunnah al-Mohammadeiah Publishers, 1953).

Ibn al-Ukhuwwah, Muhammad ibn Mohammad, *Ma'alim al-Qurbah Fi Talab al-Hisbah* (Reuben Levy, editor), (London: Gibb Memorial Series, Luzac, 1937).

Ibn Majah, *Sunan* (Cairo, 1954).

Al-Mawardi, Ali ibn Muhammad, *Al-Ahkam As-Sultaniyyah* (Beirut: Dar al-Kutub al-Ilmiyya, 1978).

Morgenstern, O., *On the Accuracy of Economic Observations*, 2nd edition (Princeton, N.J.: Princeton University Press, 1964).

Most, K. 'Accounting in France', *in* H. Peter Holzer (Ed.), *International Accounting* (New York: Harper & Row, 1984), pp. 295–314.

Qutb, Sayyid, *Al-Adalah al-Ijtim'iyah fi al-Islam* (Social Justice in Islam), (Cairo: 1953).

Schonberger, R. J. *World Class Manufacturing: The Lessons of Simplicity Applied* (New York: The Free Press, 1986).

Tawney, R. H., *Religion and the Rise of Capitalism: An Historical Study* (London: Murray, 1926).

Appendix to Chapter 3

The Fiscal Arrangements of the Early Muslim State[1]

The Revenues of the Early Muslim State

As the main text of the chapter has observed, the days of the early Islamic State are long passed, and Islam attaches no great importance to conservatism for its own sake. Nevertheless, Muslims are concerned with what was done in those times (the *Ijtihad* Period), since the practices and interpretations of the Prophet himself, and those who knew him personally, are held to enshrine the general principles of the Shari'a, which must always be observed.

Resource allocation during the early periods of Islam was a simple matter. The revenue received by the State in each year determined the amounts available for spending in the next. However, most of the resources had specific rules governing the way in which they were to be spent, and these rules were mainly directed towards fulfilling specific social responsibilities. Economic growth was hardly considered, and the budgeting policies of the State were not growth-oriented (Mannan, 1986). On the other hand, as we know, the State *was* growing very rapidly, for the most part by military conquest.

The principal sources of revenue collected by the early Islamic State were *zakah*, *kharaj*, *jizyah*, *ghanimah*, *ushoor* and *rekaaz*. Each was the subject of a separate fund account, and was disbursed according to its own set of rules. At first, the collection and disbursement was done informally, by the Prophet himself and his immediate successor, but Umar, the second *Khalifa*, established the *bait al-mal* (treasury house). This was the state treasury, through which all money and other assets received by the State were deposited, and disbursed to their various owners and beneficiaries. It follows that the *bait al-mal* handled two types of account:

1. In respect of property deposited in the treasury for safe keeping.
2. In respect of items, usually the proceeds of taxation, which were at the State's own disposal.

The charges against these accounts were also of two distinct types:

1. Liabilities for goods and services already received, such as the pay of soldiers, arms, horses and so on.
2. Payments to the various beneficiaries of the funds represented by the accounts (Mannan, 1986).

All inflows and outflows of money and property were recorded in proper books of account (Shalaby, 1983).

Bait al-mal had branch offices in each province of the Islamic State, and administered all the receipts and payments of the province. Any surpluses were transferred to the central office in the capital city, or sent elsewhere, as directed by the *Khalifa*. Initially, the provincial governor was in charge of the branch, but later the financial administration of the province was entrusted to another official, who reported directly to the *Khalifa*. The *bait al-mal* was subdivided into a number of *diwans* (departments), which administered the different types of taxation and expenditure.

Each *diwan* was required to maintain records of its financial transactions (A'gla, 1984). Together they formed the governmental accounting system of the *bait al-mal*. All sections were subject to the same regulations regarding internal control, the preservation of documents and vouchers, the preparation of annual accounts (and triennial summaries), and audit by the *diwan al-azimmah* (Al-Nuwairi, 1931; Shahata, 1950). These fairly comprehensive arrangements for compiling financial and statistical material provide for the basic principle of National Income Accounting.

The Early Forms of Taxation

One was the *diwan al-zakah*. *Zakah* was the prime source of revenue in the early state, and it has already been described at some length in the main body of the chapter. However, there are a number of features concerning its earlier administration which throw further light on how it was perceived at the time. A distinction was made between 'apparent' and 'non-apparent' property. The former consisted of animals and agricultural property, which were obvious, outwardly visible sources of wealth. The latter were gold and silver, and articles of trade, which were less obvious because they tended to be kept under cover. In the days of the Prophet Mohammed and the first two *Khalifas* the tax on both was collected officially, but subsequently Muslims were allowed to distribute the *zakah* on non-apparent property by themselves. This is seen as having established a principle whereby *zakah* can be either collected or self-administered, as the State directs. In modern times, states often collect the tax only upon a limited range of the property and income subject to it; individuals are expected to distribute the remainder personally.

Even when *zakah* was being collected personally by the Prophet, or the *Khalifa*, other people were employed to help in collecting the taxes. These tax-collectors were not always well received, and the *Khalif* Abu Bakr was forced to declare war against a number of tribes who simply refused to pay. This, and the subsequent setting up of the official *diwan*, established the further principle that all Muslims must welcome tax-collectors, and treat them courteously! More to the point perhaps, the duty extends to freely revealing the amount of the goods and income subject to *zakah*. Again, the establishment of the *diwan*, with its dual role of collecting the tax and distributing it to the beneficiaries, gives Muslims the principle of an administered system of 'social security'.

The other substantial source of early revenue was the *kharaj*. This was a land tax imposed on agricultural land which had been conquered for Islam without any resistance from its former owners. This land was called *fai'*, while the land taken by force was called *ghanimah* (war booty) and dealt with somewhat differently for tax purposes. At first, all conquered land was distributed among the warriors as *ghanimah*. However, Umar concluded that the practice was harmful, since it distracted the army from its principal duty of extending the boundaries of Islam, and also deprived the former owners of their ancestral possessions. Accordingly, *kharaj* was levied upon the *fai'* instead. The tax was fairly complicated, since it was sometimes but not always seen as attaching to the land itself—and so payable even if the owners became Muslims, or sold it to a Muslim (Al-Mawardi, 1978).

Again, the method of assessment was either proportional (*muqasamah*) or fixed (*wazifah*). The former was a share of the crop, collected after the harvest; the latter was of a fixed amount, payable on a fixed date. The method used depended upon the quality of the land, the nature of the crop, and the method of irrigation. No *kharaj* was payable if the land was uncultivated, or if the entire crop was destroyed through no fault of the owner. As has been mentioned, Umar set up a separate department, the *diwan al-kharaj*, to assess, collect and disburse both this tax and the *jizyah* tax, which we will now describe briefly. Since both taxes relate to the circumstances surrounding those who peacefully surrender to the forces of Islam, they were both known as *fai'*, and subject to the same administrative machinery.

Jizyah was a tax specifically enjoined by the Qur'an (9:29), unlike the *kharaj*. It was imposed on non-Muslims who surrendered peaceably to the Islamic forces but chose to retain their religion, while residing in the Muslim State and enjoying its protection. Such a charge was not unjust, since non-Muslims were not liable for military service and did not pay *zakah*. If they did eventually become Muslims, *jizyah* ceased to by payable, but they were, of course, liable to military service and the payment of *zakah*. *Jizyah* was not payable if, for some reason, the Islamic State was not in a position to provide protection to these people (Al-Mawardi, 1978).

Unlike *zakah* and *kharaj*, *jizyah* was levied only on adult males who were financially able to pay it. Women, children, the insane, the elderly and the destitute were specifically exempt from this tax. Priests of other religions were also exempt (Abu Yusuf, 1978). The rate of tax varied in accordance with ability to pay. In the days of the second *Khalifa*, the rich were charged 48 *dirhams* per annum, the middle class 24 *dirhams*, while the poorer people who could still support themselves paid only 12 *dirhams*. It should be noted that while this tax is mentioned in the Qur'an, the rates are not specified therein. Provision existed for the *jizyah* to be paid by instalments (Abu Yusuf, 1978). The circumstances surrounding this tax are interesting: they provide a basis for such fiscal principles as progressive taxation, and relief for aged persons and charities.

There was also a Department of Defence (*diwan al-jund*). After the introduction of *kharaj*, *ghanimah* (war booty) was confined to prisoners of war, and the property of those who opposed the armed forces of Islam in battle. The Qur'an (8:41) contains directions as to how this was to be apportioned. Eighty per cent remained with the army, as its sole official means of support; the remaining 20 per cent was divided among various beneficiaries, but latterly these were reduced to include orphans, the poor and wayfarers alone. The Appendix to Chapter 2 referred to the problems surrounding all methods of financing security forces otherwise than through direct taxation of the people for whom they provide security. It is not thought that the principles developed for *ghanimah* have any relevance to financing the security forces of a modern state.

The second *Khalifa* also introduced *ushoor* (customs duties). These were levied on the goods of non-Muslims only, and those from neighbouring states paid 10 per cent; resident non-Muslims, liable to *jizyah*, paid only 5 per cent. *Ushoor* was payable upon the entry of goods into Islamic territory; the duty was again payable if the goods remained in the country for twelve months without being sold. Goods removed from the country in one year and returned during the same year were liable to be taxed again, but goods leaving and re-entering in the same year paid no further duty (Abu Yusuf, 1978). Ships passing the harbours of the Islamic State also had to pay a 10 per cent duty on the value of their cargoes. These duties are said to have been imposed in retaliation for the similar duties levied on Muslim merchants by neighbouring states; the principles they support are those normal to this type of taxation.

There was also a tax on mines and treasure-trove, the *rekaaz* (Al-Qaradawi, 1981). This was not an important matter in early Islam, but, since it covers oil and gas reserves, as well as precious metals, the principle of this type of taxation is clearly of importance in modern Islam. If a mine or treasure-trove is discovered in the land of Muslims, the State was entitled to collect 20 per cent of the value of the material extracted, beyond a minimum quantity which did not attract taxation. Some jurists have argued that *rekaaz* (which is not referred to in the Qur'an) should be subjected to the rules of *zakah*, and pay only 2½ per cent. However, this is not a majority view (Al-Qaradawi, 1981). It should be remembered that the State has a legitimate right to nationalize such resources, if to do so were found to be in the public interest.

The revenue from *rekaaz*, together with that from the *ushoor*, and the 80 per cent of the two *fai'* taxes not devoted to charitable objects, were available for the general expenditure of the State. These were handled by the *diwan al-khatm* (office of the seal) and the *diwan al-bareed* (post office). In addition to the postal service, the latter *diwan* was also responsible for providing the chief executive of the State, the *vizier*, with intelligence reports about the social, administrative and financial affairs of the provinces (Al-Kafrawi, 1983).

Note

1. English-speaking readers will find more extensive details on this topic, and the subsequent administrative development of the Ottoman Empire, in Chapters VII and VIII of Levy (1957).

Bibliography

Abu Yusuf, Ya'qb bin Ibrahim, *Kitab al-Kharaj*, 6th edition (Cairo: Halabi Publishers, 1978).

A'gla, M., 'Al-Tatbegaat al-Tarekeyah wa al-Moua'sira li Tanzeem al-Zakah wa Door Moas-sa-satiha', *First Conference on Zakah* (Kuwait, 1984).

Al-Kafrawi, A. M., *Al-Ragaabah al-Maleeah fi al-Islam* (Alexandria: Moasa'sut Shabab Al-Gaameah, 1983).

Levy, Reuben, *The Social Structure of Islam* (Cambridge: Cambridge University Press, 1957).

Mannan, M. A., *Islamic Economics: Theory and Practice*, revised edition (London: Hodder & Stoughton, 1986).

Al-Mawardi, Ali ibn Muhammad, *Al-Ahkam As-Sultaniyyah* (Beirut: Dar al-Kutub al-Ilmiyya, 1978).

Al-Nuwairi, Ahmad, *Nihayat al-Adar fi Funun al-Adab* (Cairo: Dar al-Kutub a-Masriyah, 1931).

Al-Qaradawi, Yousif, *Figh Al-Zakah*, Vol. 1, 6th edition (Beirut: Moasa'sut Al-Re'saalh, 1981).

Shahata, L. S., 'Nizaam al-Muahasabah Ledarebat al-Zakah wu-al-Dafater al-Mustamalah fi Bait al-Mal', Master's degree thesis (Cairo University, 1950).

Shalaby, Ahmad, *Al-Igtesaad Fi Al-Fikr Al-Islami*, 5th edition (Cairo: The Renaissance Bookshop, 1983).

Chapter 4

Business Organizations and Financial Institutions within Islam

The Nature of the Entity in Islam

Chapter 1 has shown how an organization is a group of human beings who collaborate in order to obtain some advantage suggested by their perception of their environment. That chapter also demonstrated that every meta-scheme for the exploitation of conscious knowledge must contain an assumption about the 'good' which is being pursued. It follows that every business enterprise is indelibly marked with the moral implications of the metascheme which it is using. Accounting, in itself, is a neutral technique, which takes on the moral stance of the entity whose success in achieving the chosen 'good' is being measured. It seems likely that what are commonly seen as 'problems in the theory of accounting' are better described as 'problems of business organization', or even as 'problems of business morality'. This suggests that the logical development of the argument of this book requires something to be said about the application of Islamic principles to the structure of business organizations and financial institutions, before going on to the question of their most appropriate accounting theory.

In our view, the fundamental principles of Islamic business are *khilafa* and *shura*. The first lays a personal responsibility upon all Muslims for what is done with the resources entrusted to them; the second requires them to listen to the advice and grievances of those affected by what is done in their name. Together, these principles suggest that all Muslims must take a personal interest in the management of each one of the organizations in which their funds are invested, unless they are mentally or physically unable

68

to do this. It is not appropriate to make long-term investments of funds 'at arm's length' and leave their use to the discretion of other people. This requirement leads to a pragmatic, hands-on, day-to-day style on investment which is quite unlike its modern Western counterpart.

Western economics (and Western accounting theory) conceives 'business' as an abstract idea, without any detail of the personnel or technology involved. It may be that this approach has its origins in Greek and Roman society, where 'patricians' did not trade in person but left such things to slaves and freed slaves. Certainly the idea of the *rentier*, who owns economic entities and draws income from them but does not work *in* them, is of very long standing in Western society. Islam, by contrast, seems to relate everything it says about business and finance to the owner-manager.

Prima facie, this will limit the size of Islamic enterprises to what can be financed and run as a large partnership. It might seem that the massive growth of Western economic activity has been made possible through the development of joint stock companies, which has made much larger entities possible. Here, the earlier order of things is reversed. The directors, or managers, of the business trade with the 'masters'' money, without being subordinated to them. Such control as is exercised over them is that of a principal over an agent. There is a requirement to report and account, at least on an annual basis, and through general meetings to approve those reports, etc., and deal with major changes in the directors' remits to run the business.

This arrangement is at the heart of the Western joint stock company. The company is actually run by the directors, in the sense that they can buy and sell assets, initiate and close down activities, hire and discharge subordinates, and so on, at will. The shareholders have the right to receive reports, etc. from the directors, and attend general meetings of the company. The appointment of directors and the declaration of dividends, and many other important decisions regarding the company, require the consent of a general meeting.

However, the power of shareholders at these meetings is heavily circumscribed; they can only pass, or refuse to pass, motions put before the meetings by the directors. Total loss of confidence in a board which refuses to step down is not uncommon. Such situations can only be met by applications by concerned shareholders to the appropriate government departments, or the courts, for the appointment of an inspector, or compulsory liquidation of the company. In short, the ousting of directors against their will can only be achieved at considerable risk to the viability of the company.

This dictates the Western model for investor behaviour. Shareholders are essentially inactive in the running of the company; if they do not like what the directors are doing, or seem likely not to, they just dispose of their shares. The beauty of the Western stock exchange system (in this respect) is that an investor is rarely 'locked in' as a member of a public company. The efficiency of the capital market will normally supply a correct price for any share at any time. Of course, scandalous behaviour by the directors can render the shares virtually unsaleable. This is the only time when shareholders will normally attempt to exercise their rights, such as they are, in the running of the company.

This type of corporate and investor behaviour is not acceptable in Islam. Given the protection of limited liability, Western shareholders are able to enjoy the privileges of owning the company's assets without incurring the responsibility for its debts or its management. They are also able to acquire and dispose of those privileges without thought of the consequences of the change for anybody but themselves, since they do not know the identity of the vendors or the purchasers of their shares. As Chapter 2 has shown, the Shariʿa does not accept the idea of a company as an artificial person, which can be financed by one set of individuals, managed by another set, and nevertheless carry the primary responsibility for what is done in its name. It follows that the Shariʿa cannot accept the proposition that the personal responsibility of either officers or shareholders can be limited to their own misfeasances as against the company itself.

Islam and Joint Stock Companies

One of the central issues of this chapter is whether a joint stock system can operate under Islam, even in a modified form. If this is not possible, the savings of small Muslim investors cannot be mobilized in the same way as that which originally fuelled the massive economic development of the West. Nevertheless, the Qur'an contains specific exhortations to seek greater prosperity, and there seems nothing offensive in the general idea of coming together to provide the capital resources for a very large enterprise. Some part of the process of capital accumulation could come about through the Islamic banking system, whereby small depositors could share in the profits (and losses) from normal finance to industry. Finance through investment banks was a major feature of the postwar industrial development of the German Federal Republic and Japan. However, bank financing is not usually seen as a source of permanent finance for a company. A bank which made financing permanent would be turning itself into an investment trust. We will return later in the chapter to the problems of such 'institutional investment' under Islam.

The position of holding companies and subsidiaries under Islam requires discussion. The proposition that a corporation has an identity which is separable from its members is not readily accepted by Muslims. It follows that the construction of layers of such devices is seen as a method of bureaucratic organization, and nothing more. Even in those circumstances where some limitation of liability might be permissible, it is unthinkable that a group structure should be used to justify the non-payment of debts, or any other evasion of duty, by the human owners of a group which could otherwise make them good. On the other hand, the proposition that local managers might be given a legally recognized autonomy in their own areas, through the use of partially owned subsidiaries, has much to commend it under Islam. The possibility of less active partners contributing capital for exploitation by the more active has always been recognized, provided that this does not diminish the total overall responsibility of each individual partner for the whole of the undertaking.

It follows that an Islamic subsidiary can never be wholly owned, but must always contain an outside interest. If a subsidiary is wholly owned, this state of affairs merely masks the true responsibilities of the members of the holding company and puts bureaucratic obstacles in the way of full consultation between owners, managers and workers, which is the essence of Islamic management. The presence of minority shareholders within the group should cause no difficulties. Their situation is parallel to that of the Islamic bank, or other suppliers of short-term finance, with the difference that their interest is of a permanent nature. As with other loans, matters of fair dealing over transfer-pricing policy, and the restricted use of markets and suppliers, would need especial care in the case of the partially owned Islamic subsidiary.

If Islam strictly prohibits the operation of any style of joint stock company, this would seem to reduce the scope for economic development in the Islamic state to what could be financed and managed by a group of partners, perhaps with the aid of profit sharing finance from an Islamic bank. The most capital-intensive activities could only be owned by the most prosperous citizens, or by the State itself.

Nevertheless, Western business itself suggests at least two types of business organization which enable their members to combine a substantial, central corporate presence with very precise local responsibility and availability for consultations.

1. *Interlocking partnerships.* International firms of professional accountants commonly comprise a considerable number of individual partnerships at local, regional, national, continental and worldwide levels. The various levels are linked by a number of partners who are members at more than one level. An example of this arrangement is given in the Appendix to Chapter 6. There, the example is of a manufacturing concern, and it is described as a 'group'. Clearly, interlocking memberships do not constitute a group of companies in the West, in a general way. However, such arrangements could provide for the necessary degree of personal involvement over a much wider field than would be possit 'e within some unitary form of organization.

2. *Franchising arrangements.* Where a purely local service has to be supplied, but those concerned wish to make use of a national or international 'name', the benefits of national advertising and so on, franchising may provide another suitable vehicle of organization. The owner of the franchise grants local franchisees the exclusive rights to operate under the franchise name in a given area, under more or less strict conditions as to the type of service offered. Subject, as always, to the conformity of the contract with Islamic Law in general, this device seems well adapted to cases where central administration will be minimal.

Another implication of a total prohibition of the joint stock system in Islam would be the inability for an investor to withdraw his or her capital from an investment without occasioning a major upheaval in the enterprise itself. In partnerships and proprietary companies, one can only dispose of one's interest with the consent of the remaining partners, or directors. Usually, they will only permit the sale to be made to existing members, or some other people of whom they personally approve. The effect is usually to reduce the price which might be obtained for the interest, and to delay the transfer for a considerable period of time. What was said in Chapter 2 concerning the *al-Istikhara* prayer suggests that it is the duty of every Muslim to be alive to the possibility of a change in God's plan for his or her life. Of itself, there can be no virtue in restricting the speed with which a Muslim investor can dispose of an asset and acquire another, or the funds available for the new venture.

On the other hand, there are good reasons why one's fellow directors or partners would wish to control the transfer of the investment to other people. The free transferability of shares is what makes the take-over bid possible. In Western companies, at least, the inactive role adopted by the shareholders means that comparatively small acquisitions can provide a sufficient power-base to affect the control of the company. It is generally thought that a holding of as little as 5 per cent of the equity in a public company is enough to give the holder a major influence in its affairs, if only because of the possibility of placing so large a block of shares back on the market. A holding of 30 per cent is taken to provide effective (as opposed to legal) control of the company. The emergence of a new centre of power in a company can have profound effects for those who manage it, work for it, or deal with it.

Since Islam enjoins both the responsible use of wealth, and the need for consultation with others, an Islamic stock exchange cannot function with the anonymity of its Western counterparts, as will be explained in the appendix to this chapter. It might be desirable if the true name of the purchaser were known to the seller, and even whether there was an intention on his or her part to obtain control of the company. On the other hand, it would probably suffice to know that the purchaser was either a Muslim or someone domiciled in an Islamic State. The new owner of the shares would then be under an obligation to abide by the same rules of conduct as the old one. Given that, it may be that others having any relationships with the company cannot be worse off than before. Of course, the so-called 'dawn raids', whereby holdings are secretly built up by investors, are already prohibited under Islam; such behaviour is of the type of deceitful, 'cornering' activity which is part of the wider sin of *riba*.

Other features of Western capitalism encourage the ownership of assets under circumstances where one's identity cannot be discovered by others. The Swiss banking system is the best-known example, while the nearby state of Liechtenstein provides facilities for setting up trusts and other entities whose true owners and beneficiaries can never be disclosed. Even British banks offer nominee services, so the inspection of the register of members of many major public companies in the UK will only show the names of the banks who are holding the shares on behalf of customers. Of course, the City Code and other provisions of the law apply to these holdings, so one may hope that major banks do not lend their names to improper activities. Moreover, the secrecy is not absolute in the United Kingdom, where the true identities would have to be revealed to an investigator appointed by the Government, or the Stock Exchange. However, such investigations are set up only after some irregularity has been detected! Ownership under these terms is not compatible with Islam.

Further uncertainties regarding the true composition of the membership of a company arise from dealings in 'futures' in shares, and the custom of providing share options to directors and senior employees by way of an incentive. Since both futures and options will be triggered off by movements in the prices of shares, they probably run foul of the general Islamic prohibition of gambling. Convertible debentures, as such, cannot exist for an Islamic company, because of the prohibition of *riba*; however, even an agreement whereby an acceptable Islamic loan could be converted into permanent membership of the company, when the price of the shares reached a certain level, would be equally unacceptable, because the arrangement contains an element of chance.

One must conclude that while it is possible for Muslims to invest directly in companies, under conditions whereby they can liquidate their investments fairly rapidly, it is unlikely that these transfers can be made with the speed which is normal in Western countries. An Islamic business can never become the subject of a bidding 'game' played out on the floor of an exchange, or on a computer screen. The events of October 1987 suggest that the very speed and sophistication with which modern Western markets operate can be their undoing (e.g. *The Economist*, 1987). The intrinsic value of the underlying enterprises can be submerged by the floods of selling triggered off (by computers) in response to positions taken in the futures market for securities. Although similar panics have occurred on stock exchanges in Muslim countries, it would seem that these arose because investors were breaking their own religious code by trading 'on the margin'. Although a truly Islamic stock market might prove less attractive to 'savers' whose real preference was for a gamble on the stock prices, it might be expected to provide a more effective vehicle for genuine investment.

Institutional Investment and Islam

Another feature of Western financial markets which might cause concern in an Islamic context is the institutional investor, such as insurance companies, pension funds, and mutual funds. These form a very large part of the capital market in most Western countries. The concepts of insurance and pension funds as practised in the West are forbidden under Islam. This is mainly because the funds that become available under both types of scheme are invested in interest-bearing undertakings, which Islam strongly forbids.

One of the main characteristics of the practice of Islamic insurance companies is that

> the contracting parties' rights and obligations should be determined not according to what may or may not happen or take place in the future but on what is definitely guaranteed as to time and place. (Al Amin, 1986, p. 6)

This does not involve any actuarial valuations of risk. The insured is asked to pay his or her premium, which is considered as his or her contribution to the fund established by the company to meet the various contingencies. After settling all the claims that were made during the financial year and paying all management expenses, the policy-holders are entitled to share in the profits achieved according to the percentage of their contribution. However, if not enough revenue is achieved to meet the claims made during the year, the policy-holders are called upon to pay the difference.

Hence, like Islamic banks, Islamic insurance companies also work on the basis of profit-and-loss sharing. This means that risk in Islamic insurance is shared by all those who participate in the company. This is contrary to the practice of some Western 'proprietary' insurance companies, which compensate the policy-holder only for the loss which he or she incurs; whereas Islamic insurance companies indemnify their policy-holders for their loss as well as providing them with an opportunity to share in the profits that are achieved at the end of the year. Of course, in the former type, only shareholders are entitled to share in the profits. Perhaps pension funds can be established following the same philosophy of Islamic banks and Islamic insurance companies.

The concept of life assurance as practised in the West is also prohibited in Islam. As an alternative, Islamic insurance companies have developed the concept of *Al-Takaful* (the act of a group of people reciprocally guaranteeing each other) to cater for the needs of small savers whose savings are too small to be invested directly to best advantage, and who probably lack the knowledge necessary to manage their own portfolios of investments. Continued economic growth requires that these savings be mobilized into a form in which they can be invested in the capital market, under Islam as much as elsewhere.

As well as to small savers, the *Al-Takaful* scheme is also attractive to those who wish to acquire endowment life-assurance policies, which become payable in the event of a major accident, death, or at the end of a specified period, whichever occurs soonest. For example, the *Al-Takaful* scheme run by the Islamic Insurance Company in Sudan specifies that in cases where a subscriber dies before the period for which he or she has agreed to subscribe, his or her beneficiaries will receive:

1. The instalments which were not paid for the remaining period.
2. The percentage of the annual instalment which was allocated for investment, plus its share of profits, from the time the subscriber joined the scheme until his or her death.
3. The instalments of the first year, because these are not invested, and hence do not carry any entitlement to any profit.

We should consider what acceptable alternatives other than insurance companies, exist for small savers under Islam. The possible role of Islamic banks has been mentioned already, together with their current limitations as long-term sources of finance. Any company which makes long-term investments in other enterprises is a form of investment trust. A company specifically set up as an investment trust does not differ from any other holding company; its members have full responsibility for what is done in their names throughout the group they control.

Nevertheless, the mutual fund, or unit trust, might be a device which could legitimately operate under Islam. Might it be appropriate to consider small investors with no aptitude for 'big business' as the beneficiaries of some kind of trust? The issue is one of intent. This is similar to the investment deposit holders in Islamic banks who are the beneficiaries of a trust operated by the bank. On the other hand, investors in mutual funds, etc. merely deposit money with the fund in the hope that their savings will grow. Of itself, this is the sort of *rentier* activity which is anathema to Islam. However, it would not be violating the Shari'a if the surplus to be received by investors were distributed on the basis of profit-and-loss sharing.

As in all other Islamic financial institutions, those who manage Islamic mutual funds should be very strictly controlled as to the benefits and remuneration which they take from the trust. Moreover, the managers would have to be active and responsible members of the companies in which they place the investments. In this respect, they would also differ notably from their Western counterparts, who are notoriously inactive as shareholders.

It can be seen that a high moral tone is assumed to be the norm in an Islamic capital market! This is in marked contrast to the situation assumed by most Western texts on 'business ethics' (and even ethics in general), which adopt the position of a would-be honest individual in a basically corrupt world (e.g. Velasquez, 1982). Thus, they discuss the extent to which that individual can, in some way, 'consent to injustice' and still be blameless. The reasoning behind this is that more powerful forces in the enterprise can threaten the individual with economic or even personal reprisals if he or she does not 'go along'. To what extent are acts carried out 'under duress' blameworthy? These considerations have no weight in matters affecting a Muslim dealing with an Islamic company in an Islamic state, because it is assumed that everybody concerned, Muslim and non-Muslim alike, is following the requirements of the Shari'a, and that with complete sincerity of purpose.

A cynic might suppose that this assumption is unrealistic. The best that can be hoped for, one might think, is that people will see it as in their own best interest to follow the law—unless they can avoid its restrictions by force, by deceit, or by special pleading. This view assumes that Islam has only the same degree of influence on Muslims as modern Christianity has on Westerners. Chapter 2 described how business activity in the West has become detached from religious morality; the modern economizing spirit is seen as pursuing unbridled self-interest within the code of law. Religion is an optional spiritual exercise whose moral code may have some influence on the content of the law.

Muslim businessmen or women who consciously adopted this philosophy would be deluding themselves. The Qur'an (61:3) reserves its most blood-thirsty condemnations for what it calls 'dissemblers'—those who conform to the outward appearance of Islam, but entertain other motives in their hearts. Such self-delusion is not beyond possibility, and if Muslims do behave in this fashion, this book's search for a specifically Islamic theory of accounting is vain; if Muslims are not a committed people, then the same economizing philosophy can be used to model their actions as is applied to Western men and women. A Muslim would add that if Muslims are incapable of wholehearted commitment to Islam or, at worst, if an Islamic state cannot enforce strict conformity to the Shari'a, Islam is not what it claims to be—namely God's instruction manual on how to be a normal human being!

Other Collaborators in the Islamic Firm

Islam has its particular views of the needs of the other collaborators in a Muslim enterprise. In the case of creditors, it is obvious that major fixed-interest loan creditors cannot exist. All long-term finance must be of the partnership type. Even trade creditors might be expected to have wider concerns than those of finance. Muslims ought not to advance credit to those who are not expected to be able to pay—except as an act of charity. Certainly, the idea of enforcing a debt through seizure of goods or property, or insolvency proceedings, is foreign to Islam for the reasons given in the previous chapter.

The previous chapter also emphasized the *dirigiste* attitude of the Islamic State in the matter of economic planning. To this end, an Islamic enterprise must collaborate with the State through consultations and regular reports of its past performance and future intentions. Modern Islamic States are likely to impose taxes on income (for secular purposes) and therefore demand income statements in order to assess these taxes. The specifically Islamic taxation, *zakah*, is an unusually simple and well-understood tax mainly levied on property. To the extent that the Islamic State *does* collect this tax, it might have an interest in a correct statement of the tax-payer's property. However, since it is the religious duty of all Muslims to pay this tax, the State does not always collect the whole of the *zakah*. Where the tax is wholly or partly self-assessed and self-collected, a proper financial accounting statement should include information as to how the *zakah* had been distributed to those entitled to receive it.

Chapter 3 refers to the rights of the population at large (*ummah*) as the ultimate beneficiaries of the *khilafa* (viceregency or trust) in assets. Public-interest concern in corporate affairs offers one of the most obvious differences between the Muslim and the Western experience. The West recognizes the possibility of a gap between the public cost and the private cost of an activity. These 'externalities' are costs borne by the community through industrial pollution, the public provision of technical education, low-cost housing and so on, the sale of defective and harmful products, and the like. Also, there are such matters as the provision of social amenities, joint consultation, job security, and other benefits to employees. Chapter 1 relates these issues to the exercise of common sense.

These are 'grey areas', where the law does not lay down specific rights and duties. However, nowadays it is often thought that Western businesses ought to make public what they do in these matters, so that public opinion may form a view as to whether the enterprise is operated in a reasonable and socially conscious fashion. This could be seen as a further level of social control below the delegated, administrative law described in Chapter 2. One may think that it provides a particularly subtle mechanism for responding to change, by identifying areas of concern in advance of the development of specific legislative or administrative provision for their control. One might also wonder whether the calls for such information reflect a lack of confidence that Western businesses provide adequate social contacts to allow common sense to deconstruct the decisions of their managers.

Islam does not recognize the possibility of any gap between the Law and what is necessary for the proper ordering of society. It follows that Muslims cannot see any advantage to adopting higher standards of behaviour than those which the Law already enjoins upon them. This follows from the concept of Mohammed as 'the Seal of the Prophets'; the Qur'an is taken to be God's last word on every possible topic, and the deeds and sayings of the Prophet are taken as the best examples to be followed by all Muslims. There are no grey areas of Muslim behaviour. The principles for defining everybody's rights and duties in any conceivable situation are already laid down. 'Just' prices, wages and rents can be determined; other misfortunes, from whatever causes, are a matter for relief out of *zakah* (Gambling and Karim, 1986). There would be no need for specific 'social reporting', because the rights and duties of merchant and customer, employer and employee, land-lord and tenant will have been properly fulfilled. The principles of *shura* and *khilafa* could be said to ensure the proper exercise of common sense.

Senior Managers and Islam

In conclusion, something needs to be said about the role of senior managers in a Muslim company. As has been said, the directorate of a Western company behave, and are treated, much as if they were the proprietors of the enterprise. They are the agents of the company itself, rather than of the shareholders. Moreover, in the case of the largest public companies, the directors tend to be more concerned with what might be called investor-related activity, as opposed to the management of the underlying business. This involves the building up of the company through acquisitions, and defending it against bids from outside. They devise issues of stock, deben-tures, and other financial instruments incidental to these ends. This activity, and the attitudes it reflects, accords well enough with the spirit which appears to prevail among the investors who make up the market for shares in the West. The concern is to 'make money', and the making of goods and the provision of service by the underlying company is but one of the factors entering into the value of its shares on such a market.

Even the reporting of financial results, and other events, is seen as subor-dinated to the question of how 'the market' will react to the new infor-mation. Such directors see their mission as one of managing the company's cost of capital, and this includes 'managing' the price of its shares on the stock market. Their status is that of a financier, rather than an operational manager.

This chapter has suggested that take-over activity, while not impossible within Islam, may be much less common among Muslim businesses. The next chapter also suggests that the Western concept of 'a return on capital' may be dependent upon its reification through Western financial insti-tutions for its validity, rather than any intrinsic reality in the physical world. 'Investor relations' and 'the management of the cost of capital' are probably meaningless symbols, divorced from the social context in which they have been developed. A director in an Islamic company will necessarily be con-cerned with the management of real phenomena, as opposed to symbolic ones. To be sure, businesses may be acquired, new investors attracted to the company, and the cash-flows kept in balance, but these activities must be carried out with reference to specific people and objects so that the requirements for consultation and responsibility may be fulfilled.

This pragmatic approach also applies to internal aspects of management under Islam. In addition to isolating the ownership of the funds from their management, Western companies also tend to isolate their (senior) management from their production and commercial activities. This is a comparatively recent development which arose from the professional activities and writings of a number of 'management consultants' at the end of the nineteenth and the beginning of the twentieth centuries. Taylor (1911) and Fayol (1949), among others, constructed a 'management science', which was divorced from specific managerial tasks such as 'running a steel-mill' or 'running a chain of grocery stores'. Such a concept is a natural expression of the human ability to construct abstract models in the conscious mind, described in Chapter 1.

However, when that model is refined into a social and even a physical separation between 'top management' and 'the shop-floor', it also necessitates a distinctly 'Byzantine' proliferation of ritual in order to bring about its deconstruction by common sense. The modern 'world-class manufacturing' techniques, also mentioned in Chapter 1, call for the reversal of this trend. Clearly, this further dichotomy also offends against the principles of *shura* and *khilafa*. Islam would seem to require its investors to concern themselves with the physical processes of their investment, as well as the purely financial aspects of its management.

Under Islam, a senior manager who is required to exercise major, personal initiative can never be an employee. In the first place, the fiction of being the agent of a disembodied 'corporation' is not available to Muslims; principals have to be personally responsible. If the principal is in fact a minor or mentally deficient, those who manage his or her affairs are trustees (and so principals in their own right), and not agents. By contrast, it is the duty of all employees to be loyal and obedient. This follows from the general principle of *bay'a* (pledge of allegiance), which applies to every form of Islamic governance. Although obedience does not entitle Muslim employees to do anything against the teachings of Islam, they are entitled to lay responsibility for their permissible actions on the shoulders of those who gave them the orders.

It follows that Western concerns for 'industrial democracy' will have little weight under Islam. The rights and duties of employers and employees are laid down, and so are not the subject of debate in themselves. Moreover, it is the owners of the business who are ultimately responsible for what is and is not done in its name. For similar reasons, although budgetary control is central to Muslim corporate reporting it is not likely that any attention would be paid to the issues discussed in the West as 'behavioural aspects of budgeting' (e.g. Argyris, 1952; Caplan, 1966). The behaviour of managers and subordinates is prescribed by Islam, as is that of rulers and their subjects in general. Their rights and duties are guaranteed by the principles of *adalah* (justice) and *bay'a* (pledge of allegiance). It is not right for employees to play 'games of budgeting'; the absence of fear in the owner–manager–employee relationships should make them unnecessary.

It follows that all Muslim employees expect there to be someone who will give them specific orders, and tend to see the scope for personal initiative as being rather strictly confined to whatever may be necessary to achieve the objective they have been given. A senior manager, or director, could not function in a Muslim company without the status of a partner or fairly substantial shareholder. One might conclude that agency theory in general has little to contribute to any organization which has to be managed in this way.

Bibliography

Al Amin, Ahmed, M., 'Islamic Insurance', paper presented at the Conference on New Developments and Applications of Islamic Banking and Finance (Geneva: Institute for International Research, October 1986), pp. 1–11.

Argyris, Chris, *The Impact of Budgets on People* (New York: Financial Executive Research Foundation, 1952).

Caplan, Edwin H., 'Behavioral Aspects of Management Accounting', *The Accounting Review* (July 1966), pp. 496–509.

The Economist, 'What Caused the Meltdown', *The Economist*, Vol. 305 (19–25 December 1987), pp. 76–8.

Fayol, Henri, *General and Industrial Management* (C. Storts, translator), (London: Pitman, 1949).

Gambling, T. E. and R. A. A. Karim, 'Islam and Social Accounting', *Journal of Business Finance and Accounting*, Vol. 13 (1986), pp. 39–50.

Taylor, F. W., *The Principles of Scientific Management* (New York: Harper & Row, 1911).

Velasquez, M. G., *Business Ethics: Concepts and Cases* (Englewood Cliffs, N.J.: Prentice-Hall, 1982).

Appendix to Chapter 4

Islam and the Stock Exchange

Islam and Market Efficiency

It is necessary to consider whether an Islamic stock exchange would also be efficient in the economic sense. Would the prices reflect all publicly available information? This might seem unlikely at first sight, in circumstances where all existing shareholders are expected to exercise a part in the management of the enterprises they own. 'Insider trading' is always a major problem in Western stock exchanges, where directors and others who are privy to undisclosed information are under temptation to deal in the shares of their own company, or advise others to do so. Every shareholder of an Islamic company is an insider, by definition. This might not prevent market efficiency, of itself; Western directors often do hold shares in their companies, but they have to take care not to take advantage of privileged information. To that end, especial care is taken to record and monitor their dealings in their own company's shares.

The problem with a Muslim company would be that all dealings which took place while any information was privileged in this way might seem to be insider trading. Any perfect market requires equally informed buyers and sellers to be available at all times; here, it would only be the other existing members of the company who would be as well-informed as a member who wished to sell. Two consequences might be expected to follow. Outsiders might be unwilling to trade normally in any shares, but might enter the market in response to rumours and 'tips'; and the 'real' market would be limited to those with inside information, and would be very thin. Neither condition is conducive to market efficiency.

However, there may be grounds for supposing that in a typical Muslim company inside information may not always be confined to existing shareholders. We understand that the 'market' for many securities on the

University of Glamorgan
Learning Resources Centre -
Treforest
Self Issue Receipt (TR4)

Customer name: MR QINGYU XUE

Customer ID: ******3621801

Title: Business and accounting
ethics in Islam
ID: 7310795936
Due: 20/05/2013 23:59

Total items: 1
22/04/2013 15:26
Hold requests: 0
Ready for pickup: 0

Thank you for using the Self-Service
system
Diolch yn fawr

Kuwaiti stock exchanges before the recent crises of the *Al-Manakh* Stock Exchange, for example, was largely confined to members of the (extended) family which provided the management of the company (Al-Mudhaf, 1983). This may seem curious, if not undesirable to Western eyes, but follows naturally from the Islamic emphasis on succession and on social security through family support. This fact, combined with the institution of the *diwan* (social discussion group), might mean that inside information would become widely known very quickly among those who form the real market for a specific security. Insider dealing is not likely to be a problem in a market where no 'outsiders' are likely to consider buying the shares!

A preliminary study (Al-Mudhaf, 1983) has shown that at least one Islamic stock exchange did pass some of the tests of market efficiency. However, where market efficiency is brought about through an informal communications network based on family connections, it is likely that the efficiency cannot be complete. The family, however prosperous and however 'extended', is not likely to cover the full range of investments which each investor ought to consider. People will be passing up better opportunities, about which they fear they do not know enough, in favour of a more limited range for which they possess inside information. As has been said, the fragmented nature of such a market at the same time renders it liable to pure speculation based on rumour, which is, in fact, incorrect inside information.

Speculative Dealing and the Islamic Stock Market

In the nature of things, speculative trading is done 'on the margin'; even if the investor has sufficient funds to pay for the purchase, there is usually no intention to leave them in that company for any length of time. Obviously, this activity is not acceptable in Islam, which places so much emphasis on working for one's living. Also, the Islamic State has a duty to prevent occasions when a Muslim might be tempted to stray from the Shari'a. Most countries which have stock exchanges take steps to regulate them, but one would expect an Islamic State to be unusually proactive in this respect. On at least one occasion, the Kuwaiti government has intervened to make good deficiencies arising from speculative dealings on the *Al-Manakh* Stock Exchange, although on the second occasion it appears to have declined to do so (Al-Mudhaf, 1983)!

This is not to be seen as quixotic paternalism on the part of a wealthy

Arab government, merely anxious to prevent the distress likely to follow a stock exchange crash. All changes in general price levels are undesirable in Muslim eyes, since they must produce unearned 'holding gains' (and consequent non-holding losses as well). We have seen how the shares on a traditional Western stock exchange are essentially negotiable instruments, and change hands with little more formality than banknotes. Bull markets and bear markets are respectively inflationary and deflationary, unless real changes in the value of the underlying enterprises have occurred. It would follow that any Islamic State could be expected to intervene actively in its stock markets, by acting as a jobber, or market-making specialist, and supporting or damping down prices whenever the market appears to be overheating.

One might therefore expect dealings on Islamic stock exchanges to be confined to stable, long-established companies, for which one might readily form a view of what 'a sensible price' might be. This is another issue which Muslims have to consider in order to promote massive capital growth. Earlier chapters have shown that any moral code which hoped to achieve this would have to be able to accommodate change. Changes tend to involve uncertainty—and uncertainty is what makes it difficult to be sure what the sensible price of a stock may be. A new enterprise offering a new product or service has no established markets and no performance history, so its value must depend upon what success one believes it will enjoy in the future. The next chapter will show that Islam is not in favour of valuations which attempt to forecast the future, and might prefer intrinsic, current market-style valuations of realizable assets. Especially if it is to be engaged in some high-technology field, a new business is likely to possess some very bright cadres of managers, plus some largely unproven patents. Its current market value is likely to be negligible.

By contrast, small enterprises of this type have been seen as especially favoured sources of investment on Western stock markets. People have been prepared to pay large sums for new issues of equity stock in hi-tech companies. This, it is believed, has encouraged young research scientists to seek out the commercial possibilities of their discoveries, because of the comparative ease, and considerable rewards, of cashing in on the ownership of very small and untried production companies by 'going public' at an early stage. This procedure involves converting the uncertain value of their company into certainty, by passing on the uncertainty to the investing public, and so is contrary to the teachings of Islam. The fact that the investors are willing victims makes no difference; young inventors ought to develop their ideas in full, at their own risk. Further capital can be brought in from outside, of course, but as additional capital, and not to buy out the original promoters of the business.

In short, Muslims have to develop new methods that are compatible with the Shari'a and which provide incentive to the commercial exploitation of new scientific knowledge. The issue illustrates the distinction between Western growth and Islamic *tazkiyah*. Muslims might see the additional economic growth made possible by permitting essentially premature public issues of stock as not worthwhile against the spiritual damage involved, whether the venture fulfils its economic promise or otherwise. It may be that the quality of the growth encouraged by the possibility of 'cashing in' in this way may not be very high. Substantial companies of this type like IBM, for example, still retain substantial shareholdings by the original founders and their families.

An Islamic View of Mergers and Take-overs

Another feature of Western stock exchanges which provides fuel for a good deal of 'go-go' activity is the merger, or take-over bid. These should occur when an existing management is not using the company's assets to the best advantage, or where some synergy may be expected by running together two hitherto separate businesses. Some studies (e.g. Newbold, 1970) have suggested that these objectives are not often achieved; it is possible that the elimination of competition, or even the increase in directors' remuneration which results from the increased size of the unit, is sometimes the true motive for such activity. These last-named objectives are not acceptable under Islam, of course, while the need for full information and consultation over building up controlling interests in companies was discussed in the main text of this chapter.

Under these circumstances, an opportunistic, hostile bid is not likely to succeed. This may be a bad thing, if the existing directors are merely using the inertia which Islam introduces into the system in the interest of justice in order to preserve their own comfort and inactivity. However, consultation is a two-way process under Islam. Directors whose shareholders are being approached by would-be purchasers who believe they can manage the business more effectively need to consider the justice of such claims. They need to consult the whole body of existing shareholders, and not merely issue letters warning them not to accept the offer, as is commonly done in the West. Above all, they should not take covert action to frustrate the bid, either by guaranteeing the possible losses of friends who can be persuaded to bid up the price of the shares, or restructuring the company so as to make it illegal or unattractive to the bidder as an acquisition.

Bibliography

Al-Mudhaf, J., 'Kuwait Stock Market: Its Efficiency', Ph.D. thesis (University of Birmingham, 1983).
Newbold, G., *Management and Merger Activity* (Liverpool: Guthstead, 1970).

Chapter 5

An Islamic Perspective of Western Accounting Theory

The Origins of Accounting Theory

Our summary, in Chapter 2, of the history of the Christian Church's attempts to control 'the rise of capitalism' was intended to provide an indication of the issues and pressures which the Islamic revivalists are likely to encounter in applying the Shariʿa to commercial activity. As we turn to consider the implications of such a development for accounting theory, it seems appropriate to find a similar role-model in Western attempts to arrive at a set of 'Generally Accepted Accounting Principles'. This is of much more recent origin; the relevant literature goes back for barely sixty years. Oddly perhaps, the origin of this search for basic principles in corporate reporting invites a controversy similar to that over 'the Protestant Ethnic and the Spirit of Capitalism'.

It is tempting to suppose that the search originated in the aftermath of the New York Stock Exchange crash of 1929. Certainly, the specific search for 'accounting principles' by the American Institute of Certified Public Accountants was a response to a threat of state regulation to correct undesirable reporting practices, which were thought to have contributed to the artificial rise and subsequent collapse of share prices in the late 1920s. On the other hand, the later editions of Hendriksen's *Accounting Theory* (e.g. 1982) observe that a rather limited literature on such topics antedates the mid-1920s. This seems to have been occasioned by the development of 'business studies' as an academic discipline in a number of British and American universities at the turn of the century.[1] That development was itself the result of the development of 'management science', described in the previous chapter, combined with the determination of some prosperous businessmen that their new-found 'professional expertise' should have a place in university studies.

The comparatively limited success of these Western initiatives is unsurprising if one accepts what was said in Chapter 1 about the largely commonsense nature of all expertise—and the almost total absence of any consciously retained cognitive material from those in the business and accounting fields. The principles are not of a kind which are readily captured on paper! A variety of intellectual approaches have been used over the 60-year period. It may be helpful to classify them as, respectively, empirical-inductive, deductive, and information-theory based (following Whittington, 1986).

Standard-Setting and the Empirical-Inductive Approach

The empirical-inductive approach to accounting theory attempts to discover an *ex-post* rationalization as to what contemporary accounting practices aim to achieve. The process involves the development of principles and standards of accounting—the generally accepted accounting principles (GAAP)—which are meant to act as a general guide to accounting practices. In the USA, as we have said, the interaction of the American Institute of Certified Public Accountants (AICPA) and the Securities and Exchange Commission (SEC) has been instrumental in forming the various bodies that have been entrusted with the job of developing and implementing accounting principles for publicly traded organizations. In the United Kingdom, the various professional accounting bodies have also been active in the process of developing standards that regulate accounting practices. In 1973, the International Accounting Standards Committee (IASC) was formed as a result of an agreement between the leading professional accounting organizations in nine countries. IASC issues Statements of International Accounting Standards (SIAS).

In the USA, three distinct groups have been charged, successively, with the duty of regulating accounting practices. These are the Committee on Accounting Procedure (CAP, from 1935 to 1959), the Accounting Principles Board (APB, from 1959 to 1973), and the Financial Accounting Standards Board (FASB, from 1973 to the present).

The CAP followed a piecemeal approach of attacking specific problems and recommending a preferred method of accounting whenever possible (Zeff, 1972). Since it originated in the study of existing practice(s), this approach was predominantly inductive. This methodology did not find favour with some members of the American Accounting Association (AAA), who (at that time) favoured a deductive approach involving the development of accounting standards from first principles (Kohler, 1939). The failure of the CAP to provide a well-defined and structured body of accounting principles resulted in its demise and the creation of the APB.

The APB was assigned the task of developing an overarching conceptual framework which would provide a firm basis for resolving specific problems as they became evident. In addition, independent research was to be conducted into various problem areas before any pronouncements were issued. However, like its predecessor, the APB proved unable either to provide solutions for major specific reporting problems, or to set forth binding basic postulates and broad principles of accounting. More generally, it was also criticized for not broadening the 'exposure' process, so that all the interested parties could participate in the standard-setting process.

The remit to commission independent research had a particularly unfortunate outcome. Two essentially deductive studies by Moonitz (1961) and Sprouse and Moonitz (1962) were rejected, because their results were too different from the 'generally accepted accounting principles' as perceived by the APB at that time. The rejection of these studies put an end to further essays using the deductive approach, which had been called for specifically in the charter of the APB. On the contrary, the APB actually endorsed the inductive approach when it accepted Grady's study (1965), which attempted to discover the basic concepts underlying accepted accounting principles, on the basis of a study of accepted principles and practices in the field.

The FASB—a semi-independent organization—has succeeded the APB in the task of establishing and improving standards of accounting. Perhaps the most challenging work undertaken by FASB is the continuing project of developing a 'conceptual framework'. According to FASB, the purpose of the conceptual framework is to establish objectives and concepts to be used in the development of accounting standards, as an aid in the preparation of financial statements, and to increase the user's understanding and confidence in financial statements. In other words, the conceptual framework is to act as a constitution, which would lay down broad goals and policies that would serve as a foundation for the development of a cohesive set of accounting standards for all purposes. However, doubts have been voiced (e.g. Dopuch and Sunder, 1980) as to the usefulness of a conceptual framework in providing answers to complex problems where there are dissimilarities of objectives among interested parties. Moreover, the conceptual framework is based on the short-range economic consequences of providing information, and not on the more basic objectives of social and economic consequences (Hendriksen, 1982). In that respect, the research methodology being adopted differs markedly from the inductive and deductive approaches preferred by the earlier bodies. The FASB has ceased to concern itself with the discovery of some transcendental *principles of accounting* in favour of finding *reporting practices* which will lead to the making of optimal decisions by accounts users. This 'information-theory' approach will be discussed in Appendix II of this chapter.

In order to meet some of the criticisms levelled at its predecessors, the FASB has introduced changes in the standard-setting process which are aimed at increasing the participation of its constituency. This involves giving consideration to the views of the various user groups whose economic interests may be affected by the implementation of a certain standard. In other words, emphasis was given to the (short-range) economic consequences of accounting decisions and accounting standards (see Zeff, 1978). However, while this system of due process has enabled user groups to play an active role in setting standards, the lobbying to safeguard the FASB's own vested interest has meant that accounting standard-setting is inevitably a political process (Horngren, 1973; Solomons, 1978; Kelly-Newton, 1980; Hope and Gray, 1982). This indicates that the standard-setting process is a matter of social choice (Horngren, 1981).

These political and social aspects of the standard-setting process accord with what was said in Chapter 1 about the high common-sense element in accounting. It also explains the unresolved problems of finding the most appropriate research methodology in this field. In general, research is aimed either at model construction, or the logical closure of an earlier model. Modelling belongs to our conscious intelligence, so it is important that our models are not 'contaminated' by common sense, as defined. They must stand or fall by their conscious, often mathematical closure. Common sense should only be used *subsequently* to the adoption of some model, to deconstruct it.

The political lobbying within the FASB is the ritual through which its models are, quite properly, deconstructed. The process is only problematic because it involves open and (anthropocentrically speaking) non-rigorous dissent from an apparently validated model. It has been argued (Gambling, 1984, Chapter 4) that this approach to standard-setting secures the worst of available results. The process of commissioned research, exposure drafts, and the issuing of 'definitive' standards differs from that of 'delegated legislation, or administrative law' (see Chapter 2) in several vital respects. The standards do not have the full force of law—and they are not the subject of day-to-day negotiation and amendment. Above all, none of these Western or Westernized bodies has been able to arrive at the necessary basic principles against which individual problems can be adjudicated.

Although the empirical inductive approach does not commend itself to Islam, it is likely that a similar political process would accompany the establishment of Islamic accounting standards. The fact that different user groups continue to lobby for their vested interests in the process of setting Islamic accounting standards would not be seen as attempts to evade the Shari'a principles. The principles of *shura* and *adalah* endorse the right to be heard. For this reason, Islamic jurists would be expected to play an influential role in debates over which financial reporting system should be implemented, and their various views might favour particular user groups. Their expertise would nevertheless ensure that all the arguments advanced remained in conformity with the precepts of the Shari'a. Thus, there are good grounds for arguing that in an Islamic context the process of setting accounting standards would certainly be a political one, but its outcome would never be a matter of social choice. It also follows that while the financial consequences of accounting standards would always be of significance to the individual user groups, the principles of *khilafa* and *tazkiyah* would compel them to listen to arguments on behalf of the *ummah*, or society at large. Above all, the principles of *bay'a* would ensure their unfeigned compliance with the eventual form of the regulation.

In conclusion, we can see that the empirical-inductive approach to accounting theory represented the accounting profession's own attempts to extract a coherent theory from what it perceives itself as doing, or perhaps perceives that it ought to do. To the extent that neither of these perceptions *was* based on any one principle, the results were seen to be less than satisfactory. A mixture of epigenetic drives, utilitarian rationalism and confused ideas of fair practice could not produce the coherent code of generally accepted accounting principles which those earlier accounting theoreticians sought.

An Islamic View of the Empirical-Deductive Approach

Nevertheless, the approach of *ex-post* rationalization of practice has resulted in the development of a number of accounting concepts. These concepts are variously called principles, axioms, postulates, assumptions and rules. Following the implementation of accrual accounting, accountants tended to pursue certain implicit rules in exercising professional judgements in the recording and reporting of economic transactions (Henderson and Peirson, 1983). Several research projects (e.g. Sanders *et al.*, 1938; Gilman, 1939; Littleton, 1953) were conducted with a view to identifying the concepts which underlay accounting practices. The result was the basic accounting concepts which form the basis for historical cost accounting. For example, ideas such as objectivity, matching and realization are rationalizations of the use of the historical cost method, while other doctrines such as materiality and conservatism provide justification for some practical departure from its use.

The use of historical cost for asset valuation is justified basically by the concept of conservatism. Sterling states:

> Cost is not a fundamental tenet of accounting; instead it is a derivative of the conservatism principle of valuation. (Sterling, 1967, p. 111)

A number of rulings cast doubt on the relevance of the concept of conservatism for Islamic financial reporting. Many of these relate to the *zakah* tax, whose nature and method of assessment have been described in Chapter 3. For example, the valuation of inventories and marketable equity securities (interest-bearing debt securities are not allowed in Islam) on the basis of net realizable value for *zakah* purposes would mean that no consideration could be given to the lower of cost or market rule. Moreover, a debt is not excluded from the base on which *zakah* is calculated until it is established that it cannot be collected (Al-Qaradawi, 1981). This would mean that only specific bad debts should be deducted from accounts receivables in the calculation of *zakah*, and allowances for doubtful debts would not be deductable. Adherence to the concept of conservatism would lead to understatement of the funds that · ould be subject to *zakah*. It would not be an acceptable practice to use one valuation for the *zakah* calculation and another for other reporting purposes, since this would imply a division between matters of religion and business affairs.

The use of the concept of conservatism to justify deliberate underestimation of net assets and profits is not to be desired among Muslims, in a general way. The determination of the true wealth of each person is a necessity in Islam since it enables Muslims to adhere to the warning in the Qur'an against miserliness: 'And ye love wealth with inordinate love' (Qur'an 89:20). For example, in an Islamic bank, unbiased valuation rules would need to be followed to report the appropriate wealth of shareholders, as well as those of other groups (such as investment deposit holders) who have a major vested interest in the bank (because they share in its profits and losses).

The going-concern assumption is seen as providing another basic support for the utilization of historical costing in Western accounting. Accountants assume that an entity will survive long enough to carry out its commitments and fully realize its existing assets in its present line of business. This presumption is used mainly to justify:

1. The adoption of current–non-current classification of assets and liabilities.
2. The use of the historical cost of fixed assets as prepayments of expenses which can be matched against revenue for income measurement purposes.

From an Islamic perspective, neither reason is relevant. The primary purpose in classifying assets as current and non-current is to identify the wealth which is subject to *zakah*. This is important because *zakah* is assessed only on wealth acquired for trading (i.e. net working capital including cash) and not on wealth procured for utilization (i.e. fixed assets) (Shahata, 1970). For this purpose, current and non-current assets are classified by reference to the *zakah* period (one lunar year). The former are intended to be consumed, sold, or converted into cash during the *zakah* period, while the latter are to be retained beyond that time.

The equation of fixed assets with prepaid expense offends against the requirements for true valuation of wealth (whether or not it is subject to *zakah*) and for openness to change.

The preparation of financial information for *zakah* purposes would also involve periodicity assumptions, as can be seen in the discussion of the going-concern principle. In traditional Western accounting, the periodicity assumption is justified on the basis that the users of financial statements cannot wait until the end of a firm's life before the success of its operations is measured. Primacy is placed on the relevance of the financial reporting at the expense of its objectivity. The periodicity assumption has led to the development of accruals accounting, and the principles of income recognition and matching.

In Islamic accounting, a similar assumption of periodicity would be justified on totally different grounds. As we have seen, one whole lunar year should elapse before any wealth could be liable to *zakah*. Accounting statements would, therefore, be prepared for that particular period, showing the amounts on which *zakah* would be levied.

In Islam, the approach and process of developing accounting standards would be very different. Basically, an *ex-post* rationalization of accounting practices would not be acceptable, because there is no evidence that what is being practised is necessarily compatible with the principles of Islam. Indeed, this most certainly would be the case given the separation between spiritual and temporal affairs of life in the West, and the spread of that phenomenon to the Muslim countries as shown in the Appendix to Chapter 2.[2]

An Islamic View of the Deductive Approach

Although the empirical-deductive approach has been the source of the various principles we have discussed, it will be remembered that many Western practitioners and academics would have preferred the deductive approach.

The earliest efforts of this sort involved attempts to bring the accountants' concept of profit into line with the economists' ideal of a theoretical 'true income' measurement. All these measurement schemes require *some* valuation of future streams of income; the accounting theorists have seen their task as one of finding reliable, objective 'surrogates' for these valuations, which remain highly subjective until the enterprise is finally liquidated! One must enquire as to whether Islamic 'income' is dependent upon the uncertainties of future events.

It could be argued that the *zakah* valuations determine asset valuations for all purposes. If so, the 'true *Islamic income*' of any enterprise would be established beyond argument. On the other hand, *all* taxation systems lay down some required methods of valuation of assets. Moreover, in many countries, deductions cannot be charged in arriving at taxable income unless they are treated in the same way in both the tax computation and the regular financial statement of the enterprise.

This practice is not followed in the English-speaking world, where discrepancies between reported profits and taxable profits are completely acceptable (SSAP, 1985). To the extent these represent reversible 'timing differences' in the incidence of costs, their effect is recognized as a 'reserve for deferred taxation'. This represents an existential approach to income determination. Income might be a different figure for different purposes; perhaps the *ex-ante* 'true income' *is* a different figure for different people, depending on their attitude to risk. If so, all that is required is that what they report as their income should be *reasonable*. It is for the recipients of the financial statements to decide whether they want to accept the given valuations.

At the outset, it is necessary to consider whether the concept of 'economic profit' could ever be a proper goal for Islamic accounting, if it could be shorn of one or two more unacceptable features. This has certainly been the view of some Islamic scholars, who argue that

> apart from specific differences . . . the Islamic approach is very near to the Western approach in so far as the application of accounting conventions and principles is concerned. *Accounting postulates . . . all apply to the Islamic approach* (El-Ashker, 1987, p. 199, emphasis added).

We believe that these unacceptable features are so fundamental to Western deductive theory that their removal would render any contribution to Islamic theory of minimal significance. For example, Western theory's most concrete representation arises as 'the economic rate of return on capital'. This is the rate which reduces the cash-flows from an investment over its life to the amount of original investment. The value of the investment at an intermediate point is simply the value, at that time, of the subsequent remainder of the flows. One must first enquire as to whether the calculation of a rate of return on investment is, of itself, in breach of the injunction against *riba*, or usury.

The sin of usury consists in receiving *or paying* a sum of fixed interest on a loan, which varies in proportion to the time it is outstanding. *Prima facie*, return on investment is neither received nor paid, but merely describes the mathematical relationship between the original investment and the net income which arises from it. However, the nature of the model which links the investment to the income is such that sums of money-in-the-future are said to be less valuable than the same sums of money-in-hand. In short the calculation assumes that money has a time-value.

This assumption is now a part of modern Western culture, as we have seen from Chapter 2. For Muslims, the time value of money does not exist. Any interest charge, however small, is therefore at best a sort of insurance—against the failure of the debtor, or even a fall in the value of the currency. Every Muslim is expected to bear with his or her own share of whatever misfortune God may send.

It might be thought that disbelief in the time-value of money is on a par with disbelief in gravitational force. Those who do not accept the facts of life must, one might think, be worse off as a result. However, the concept of return on the capital needs some strict conditions in order to work. For example, after the original (negative) investment, all subsequent net flows must be positive; if this is not so, there may be no unique rate that will discount the flows back to the original investment.

Also, the discounting factor itself must be positive. That is to say, there can be no circumstances in which it *would* be preferable to have $1 later than $1 now. This assumption rests on further strong assumptions about the returns on capital that will be available for investments to be made at those times when the cash-flows fall in. We have seen that Islam does not encourage the use of very long time horizons.

Above all, the concept of the time value of money assumes that there truly is an effective market for future income streams. This is an example of the institutional 'outward and visible sign' of a ritual which was noted in Chapter 1. In the West, such people exist, and there are institutional facilities to bring buyers and sellers of future income together. Elsewhere, they commonly do not exist, so returns on capital—and economic profit—are strictly meaningless.

Economic anthropology tells us how people do rank investments in the absence of an operational system of evaluating future income. They consider the cash-flows themselves, and how these mesh in with their own personal needs and uses for cash (Acheson, 1972). This is how people run their own private affairs, even in the West; when buying a house, they rarely consider 'What is the mortgage interest-rate?', but rather 'Can I afford the payments?'.

Again, the concept of return on capital assumes that the enterprise is capable of (infinite) expansion without invalidating the model. Common sense tells us this cannot be the case. For example, a beggar selling matches in the street has a wonderful return on capital, but is still miserably poor. Why do not venture capitalists pour investments into these match-sellers? Clearly, many of them simply could not run a larger business, but even those who could are unlikely to be able to sell large numbers of matches and still earn their original return!

Even so, there are many investments with the features which permit their meaningful analysis in terms of return on capital. Moreover, conventional accounting techniques capture their overall performance well enough (Kay and Mayer, 1986). However, this type of investment is precisely the arm's-length, inactive, *rentier* method of employing capital which is not favoured by Islam, which prefers active managerial participation in a partnership of the types described in Chapter 4.

In short, the concept of a rate of return on investment is not so much contrary to Islam[3] as opaque to Muslims. However, there are other serious problems with the concept. *Ex-post* economic profit is 'smoothed'—it is a regular percentage of the diminishing capital value of the investment. There are no good or bad years: the investment project is viewed as a whole, across its entire life. Some might suppose that this aspect of the concept accords well enough with Islam. A Muslim's fortune is predestinated by God. The ancient Greeks had an outwardly similar idea when they said 'Call no one fortunate until they are dead'. Obviously, both ideas postpone the *ex-post* reckoning for a very long time.

However, Greek stoicism considered Man as the random plaything of the gods, and so might have commended the efforts of accountants to find satisfactory surrogate measures of 'wealth' which were based upon best approximation of what the future might bring. The question of whether Islam induces a similar fatalistic approach to life was mentioned in the Appendix to Chapter 2, where it was concluded that Islam's predisposition to fatalism was no greater than that of Christianity.

Islamic obedience is an acceptance of God's current will. Men and women are not required, or encouraged, to second-guess God about His future will. Indeed, it is commonly held that time itself has no meaning for God; thus He always watches someone do something contrary to His will, but never predestinates him or her to do it! On the other hand, it is not appropriate to do nothing about the future, as humans see it. People need to place themselves in the best possible position to cope with God's will as it reveals itself to them.

Thus far, we have considered the Islamic response to Western deductive theories of accounting, which are based on economic theory. It would be appropriate to say something about the more recent and much slimmer body of accounting theory which has sought to deduce accounting theory from other parts of the social sciences. The contribution from social psychology to Western theory has already been discussed. It has little relevance for Muslims; Islam is at war with 'the lower human nature', and simply requires its followers to observe a higher code of behaviour.

Another line of deductive reasoning has been through philosophy and anthropology. This would include Gambling's *Societal Accounting* (1974) and the writings of what might be called 'the Sheffield School' (e.g. Chua *et al.*, 1981; Lowe and Tinker, 1977). These ideas underlie much of what was said in Chapter 1.

Other writers have been influenced by ideas from sociology and political science (e.g. Tinker, 1985). Accounting provides a confirmation of an existing power structure. As we observed in Chapter 1, this may well be the primitive epigenetic purpose of accounting; any social group more elaborate than an ant-hill or a tribe of baboons needs a system for distributing its surpluses, and a way of expressing debtor/creditor relationships. Whether this is seen to be a good thing or a bad thing will depend upon one's view of the justice of that power structure—and perhaps its efficiency in coping with a changing environment.

In a general way, social orders tend to be rather conservative. The rich stay rich and the poor stay poor, unless extremes of indolence or activity, backed by good or bad fortune, bring about change. Again, as we have seen, Islam teaches a distinctly limited form of conservatism. The poor should do their best to live within their means, while the rich have a duty to live *up to* their means. The whole drift of the Shariʿa is against the accumulation of capital; indeed, the *zakah* and the Muslim rules of inheritance promote the wider distribution of wealth.

It may be that there are not the points of conflict between Islam and these other social sciences that exist between it and Western neoclassical economic theory. This is because social psychology, anthropology and sociology adopt more truly positive approaches to human behaviour. They are mainly descriptive, and tend to produce rather tentative models to explain the phenomena they observe. They mostly lack the normative (affirmative) element which is so noticeable a feature of economic theory.

For the more general type of business activity, it would seem that return on capital and economic profit are inimical to the teachings of Islam on more than one count. They also lack that compelling operational force which suggests that those concepts have value as an ideal to which accounting theory and practice should aim, as will be explained in the second appendix, to this chapter.

An Islamic Theory of Valuation

By contrast, Muslims have to abide by the Shariʿa in both the social and the economic aspects of their lives. This means that they would tend to follow a normative deductive approach in setting accounting standards. This involves deducing the objectives of financial reporting, the postulates of accounting, and the definitions of concepts from Shariʿa principles. These objectives, postulates and concepts would constitute the foundation of a structural framework which would act as a reference for the development of principles for accounting.

In short, Muslims would expect to be able to deduce generally accepted accounting principles from Shariʿa principles, notwithstanding the failure of Western attempts to deduce them from economic ones. This follows the conclusion in the final paragraphs of Chapter 1. Islam does not admit that there is a distinction to be drawn between what is 'good for business' and any other sense of 'the Good'. Muslims would argue that Western inability to formulate 'Generally Accepted Accounting Principles' proceeds from the Western desire to justify that dichotomy. Some Western writers have commented adversely on this deficiency (e.g. Briloff, 1972). Chapter 4 has shown how Islam discourages ambiguity and disingenuity in business. For example, accounting for capital leases is only a problem where it is thought right to create leases as legal fictions for tax avoidance or 'window-dressing' purposes. Similarly, controversies over pooling versus consolidation of group results lose their meaning in a system where groups of companies cannot exist, other than in the form of common share holdings with *bona fide* commercial purposes.

Again, questions of asset valuation can only arise where the supposed pursuit of economic profit involves essentially circuitous assessments of their profit-earning capacity. We shall show how Islam has always indicated more pragmatic methods of valuation. This Shari'a framework for financial accounting would be considered as part of the social and economic systems of Islam which ultimately lead to the one goal of worshipping God in the way He prescribed.

Issues of asset valuation are well-established by the Shari'a principles dealing with *zakah*. Chapter 2 stated that *zakah* is one of the five pillars of Islam, and its calculation and payment is a duty which Muslims have to fulfil. Accounting has a significant role to play in providing information to enable business organizations to determine the amounts liable to *zakah*. This is one of the major objectives of the financial statements of Islamic organizations. Current cost accounting and, in particular, net realizable value are used for net current assets valuation in the calculation of *zakah* as explained in Chapter 3 (Al-Qaradawi, 1981).

As has been observed, Muslims are encouraged neither to dwell upon what is past, nor to speculate unduly about the future. The *khilafa* principle and the spirit of the *al-Istikhara* prayer enjoin an openness to God's will and whatever it may require of the believer. The possibility of an urgent need to realize existing assets in order to acquire others is always before a Muslim, and his or her assessment of their value (and of the income they generate) should reflect this fact.

Although it was not devised with Islam in mind, a very suitable method of valuation would be that advocated by Chambers (1966), known as 'Continuously Contemporary Accounting' (CoCoA). In essence, this relies on the fact that a market exists for a wide range of land and buildings, used and new plant, equipment and vehicles, finished and partly finished merchandise. Moreover, it is not difficult to discover the prices ruling on those markets at any time, if the goods are dealt in at all frequently. One might say that if it is not easy to obtain prices of this sort for any asset, one would almost certainly experience difficulty in selling it all, at short notice.

One important condition which Chambers places on the assets which are to be valued in this way is that they are separable. That is to say, their price is not some arbitrary part of the price of a larger set or group of items; it is the price of the item sold as a separate, individual unit. As Chambers argues the point, the enhanced value of a set of antique chairs over that of an individual chair is akin to the goodwill of a business. It looks toward the use of the item in the future. Goodwill itself has no value under this philosophy; it is not saleable as a separate item from the assets to which it relates.

Obviously, the goodwill or some more specific know-how of a business may be valuable. However, it has no value whatsoever as a resource contributing to flexibility toward every possible change of plan. This is because it can only be realized if the proposed change calls for the disposal of the whole enterprise, or a major part of it. In the same way, extremely costly and potentially very valuable assets may sometimes have no readily available market-quotation. Such items as oil refineries, major electricity generating plants, highly specialized computers, very large presses and profiling-machines, and so on cannot often be sold as individual pieces of equipment. They have much in common with goodwill: they are not really saleable, except as part of the whole enterprise. Their value in the event of some change of direction which stays short of total disinvestment is negligible.

On the other hand, the valuation of current assets on the basis of net realizable values for *zakah* purposes does mean that recognition is given to unrealized profits resulting from difference between the cost and market values of inventories and marketable equity securities. This is in conformity with the rulings in the Shari'a, which states that while both realized profits and holding gains on current assets are liable to *zakah*, only the former could be distributed (Attia, 1984). The issue will be discussed again later, as part of our exposition of a specifically Islamic concept of wealth and income.

Since *zakah* is mainly assessed on wealth, it is the balance sheet which would provide the main source of accounting information. Consideration would also be given to the realizable values of dues and prepayments pertaining to the *zakah* period, which would support the use of a form of accrual basis in Islamic accounting.

Unlike conventional Western accounting, an accounting system based on the *zakah* calculation emphasizes the significance of real assets and accordingly analyses all transactions in terms of their effect on assets, liabilities and owners' equity. As will be shown below, an examination of what constitutes growth of wealth, from an Islamic perspective, would help to explain the shift of focus from a revenue-expense approach to an asset-liability approach for income measurement purposes. Under the latter approach, emphasis would be placed on the definition, recognition and measurement of assets and liabilities, while revenue recognition and matching principles would become less significant.

In measuring income, conventional Western accounting uses the revenue-expense approach as the basic orientation of current financial reporting practices. This approach concentrates on the flow of funds through the business and makes use of concepts of revenue recognition and matching principles to guide the identification and measurement of revenue and expenses and then establish arbitrary methods to match them. These enable accountants to analyse and measure the flow between capital and revenue, and income and expenses.

Profit is measured according to a concept of capital maintenance, although it has been argued in Chapter 1, that this practice does not usually correspond to actual policy in the matter. It is seen as important to differentiate between the return *on* capital and the return *of* capital, although the desire to do so may be neurotic in origin. Thus, before any profits are available to be paid out as dividends, money capital should be maintained intact.

Historical cost accounting can achieve this result by amortizing the cost of fixed assets over their lives. It is obvious that the provision of depreciation before arriving at divisible profit does not (of itself) ensure that liquid funds are available to replace the assets at the end of their lives. The funds could have been applied elsewhere. In any case, the total historical cost of an asset is rarely the precise sum needed to replace it. The item may not be directly replaced at all. Even where a recognizable replacement is acquired, its money-price will usually be different, by reason of technological change, or changes in the purchasing power of the currency itself.

The problems experienced in the West over maintaining capital in times of severe inflation arise from deficiencies in Western approaches to wealth and income, which attempt to match historical cost and revenue. CoCoA is not affected in this way, as Chambers has observed (1969, 1976). Islam would favour a similar method of valuation. We shall see that the Islamic approach is different in several respects from its Western counterpart, and is not affected by changes in purchasing power. The first appendix to this chapter says something of the Muslim attitude toward inflation.

Although the revenue-expense approach has been dominant in accounting practice, there are signs which suggest a change of focus to the asset-liability approach. This is evident in FASB's definition of income as

> the change in equity of an entity during a period of transactions and other events and circumstances from nonowner sources. (Financial Accounting Standards, Board, 1980, paragraph 56)

The Islamic approach to income measurement is of this type. One of the features of *zakah* is that it is assessed primarily on wealth; this has the capacity to grow, irrespective of whether it has produced a profit or a loss (Al-Qaradawi, 1981). From an Islamic perspective wealth can grow as a result of:

1. *Profit*: realized gains resulting from the sale of current assets;
2. *Gil'ah*: unrealized gains resulting from the increase in the value of current assets; or
3. *Fa'edah*: realized and unrealized holding gains on fixed assets (Attia, 1984).

However, not all growth is subject to *zakah* or can be distributed as income. For the purposes of the former, only growth in the form of realized and unrealized gains on current assets is included in the calculation of *zakah*, while only growth in terms of realized gains on current and fixed assets can be distributed as income. The latter ruling would appear to endorse the concept of capital maintenance, but this is only indirect support for that highly abstract concept. The Shari'a principle involved here is simply the duty to settle one's debt; *gil'ah* and *fa'edah* are not available to meet the claims of creditors!

The importance attached to tangible saleable assets as a base for the calculation of *zakah* and the determination of income that can be distributed reflects the importance attached to the corporate pragmatism noted in Chapter 4. This is why the asset-liability approach is suitable to the needs of all users of Islamic financial reporting. This is in direct contrast to the conventional Western accounting principles, which are developed to satisfy the information needs of what Whitman and Shubik (1973) call investor psychology. According to this view, investors are not directly interested in what is going on in the business and do not care to analyse its underlying value. Instead, (it is assumed) they are concerned mainly with market analysis. Such a perspective would not be acceptable in Islam, in any case. Muslim stockholders have a responsibility to know what is taking place in the organization in which they are investing, for the reasons given in Chapter 4.

The entity concept is another basic assumption of conventional Western accounting. It views the business organization as an entity separate from its owners. In accounting, a number of theories have attempted to describe the relation between the organization and its owners. According to the proprietary theory, the firm's owners are the focus of attention. While a firm is considered by law to be an entity separate from its owners, the proprietary theory advocates the view that the firm is an instrument of the owners. The assets of the firm belong to them and its liabilities are their obligations. In this context, accounting plays the role of determining the net worth of the owners. Hence the importance of the balance sheet as a major source of information. Again the discussion in Chapter 4 on the nature of the Islamic enterprise would indicate the use of the proprietary theory, as does the need to account for *zakah* on the value of the stockholders' share of the corporate assets. Since the tax varies with specific types of assets, the market price of the stock itself would not be appropriate for this purpose.

One of the basic conditions of *zakah* is that it is levied on individuals who are Muslims. Entities (as such) are not liable to *zakah*. Instead, it is the owners who are responsible for finding out the value of their net assets at the end of the *zakah* period, and so become able to determine the amount that they should pay out as *zakah*. The accounts should provide the information required by shareholders to fulfil that duty. Given this relationship between the owners and the organization's assets, it would be superficial to consider the latter as having a separate personality.

Another Western accounting practice which does not accord with Islamic accounting is the convention of distinguishing between the economic substance and the legal form of transactions, when the substance is given preference over the form. This is also the case with the convention of industry practice. The peculiar nature of certain industries (such as oil and gas) would not justify departure from the rules of the Shari'a, for reasons explained in Chapter 4. The Western accounting problems which both conventions are designed to remedy arise only because Western business people are able to organize their enterprises in ways which offend against the Shari'a principles.

This discussion suggests that the conceptual framework of accounting currently applied in the West finds its justification in a dichotomy between business morality and private morality. As such, it cannot be implemented in other societies which have revealed doctrines and morals that govern all social, economic and political aspects of life.

Islam has its own cohesive rules which dictate how a business should be run. These rules can be applied at any time and in any culture. Accounting theory and practice have to pursue these rules if they are to be of any relevance to obedient Muslim users.

Notes

1. Typically, a Chair of Accounting and a Chair of Commerce were among the foundation chairs established when the University of Birmingham was created in 1905. This university was formed from the amalgamation of local technical and medical schools, largely through the efforts of Joseph Chamberlain, a prominent local and national figure in British political and industrial life at that time.
2. Nevertheless, the recently established Islamic financial institutions have employed Islamic jurists in order to ensure that all business transactions are carried out in accordance with the Shari'a precepts. Accounting standards might be induced from the practice of these institutions, because their practice is already in conformity with the Shari'a.
3. Tomkins and Karim (1987) have reached the same conclusion.

Bibliography

Acheson, J. M., 'Accounting Concepts and Economic Opportunities in a Tarascan Village: Emic and Etic Views', *Human Organization*, Vol. 31 (1972), pp. 83–91.

Attia, Mohammed Kamal, *Mouhaasabat Al-Sharikaat-wa-Al-Masarif Fi Al-Nizam Al-Islamia* (Accounting for Companies and Banks in an Islamic System), (Cairo: Dar Al-Gamiaat Al-Masria, 1984).

Briloff, Abraham J., *Unaccountable Accounting* (New York: Harper & Row, 1972).

Chambers, R. J., *Accounting, Evaluation and Economic Behavior* (Englewood Cliffs, N.J.: Prentice-Hall, 1966).

—— 'Price Variation Accounting: A General Notation', in R. J. Chambers, *Accounting, Finance and Management* (Sydney: Arthur Andersen and Butterworths, 1969), pp. 636–42).

—— 'Whatever Happened to CCE?', *The Accounting Review*, Vol. LI (1976), pp. 385–90.

Chua, W. F., R. C. Laughlin, E. A. Lowe and A. G. Puxty, 'Four Perspectives in Accounting Methodology', unpublished paper (University of Sheffield, 1981).

Dopuch, Nicholas, and Shyam Sunder, 'FASB's Statement on Objectives and Elements of Financial Accounting: A Review', *Accounting Review* (January 1980), pp. 1–21.

El-Ashker, Ahmed Abdel-Fattah, *The Islamic Business Enterprise* (London: Croom Helm, 1987).

Financial Accounting Standards Board, 'Elements of Financial Statements of Business Enterprises', *Statements of Financial Accounting Concepts No. 3* (1980).

Gambling, T., *Societal Accounting* (London: Allen & Unwin, 1974).

Gambling, T., *Positive Accounting: Problems and Solutions* (London: Macmillan 1984).

Gambling, T. E., and R. A. A. Karim, 'Islam and Social Accounting', *Journal of Business Finance and Accounting*, Vol. 13 (1986) pp. 39–50.

Gilman, Stephen, *Accounting Concepts of Profit* (Ronal Press, 1939).

Grady, Paul, 'Inventory of Generally Accepted Accounting Principles for Business Enterprises', *Accounting Research Study No. 7* (New York: AICPA, 1965).

Henderson, Scott, and Graham Peirson, *Financial Accounting Theory: Its Nature and Development* (Melbourne: Longman, 1983).

Hendriksen, Eldon S., *Accounting Theory*, 4th edition, (Homewood, Ill.: Irwin, 1982).

Hope, Tony, and Rob Gray, 'Power and Policy Making: The Development of an R and D Standard', *Journal of Business Finance and Accounting*, Vol. 19 (1982), pp. 531–58.

Horngren. Charles T., 'The Marketing of Accounting Standards', *Journal of Accountancy* (October 1973), pp. 61–6.

—— 'Uses and Limitations of a Conceptual Framework', *Journal of Accountancy* (April 1981), pp. 86–95.

Kay, J. A., and C. P. Mayer, 'On the Application of Accounting Rates of Return', *The Economic Journal*, Vol. 96 (1986), pp. 199–207.

Kelly-Newton, Lauren, *Accounting Policy Formulation: The Role of Corporate Management* (Reading, Mass.: Addison-Wesley, 1980).

Kohler, Eric L., 'Theories and Practice', *Accounting Review* (September 1939), pp. 316–21.

Littleton, A. C., *Structure of Accounting Theory* (Sarasota, Fla.: American Accounting Association, 1953).

Lowe, E. A., and A. M. Tinker, 'Sighting the Accounting Problematic: Towards an Intellectual Emancipation of Accounting', *Journal of Business Finance and Accounting*, Vol. 4 (1977), pp. 263–76.

Moonitz, Maurice, 'The Basic Postulates of Accounting', *Accounting Research Study No. 1* (New York: AICPA, 1961).

Al-Qaradawi, Yousif, *Fiqh Al-Zakah* (The Jurisprudence of Zakah), Vol. I, 6th edition (Beirut: Moasasat Al-Rysaalh, 1981).

Sanders, Thomas H., Henry R. Hatfield and Underhill Moore, *A Statement of Accounting Principles* (Sarasota, Fla.: American Accounting Association, 1938).

Shahata, Shawgi Ismail, *Mohaasabat Zakat Al-Mal: Illman-wa-Amalan* (Accounting for Zakah Wealth: Concepts and Practice), (Cairo: Maktabat Al-Anglo Al-Massriyah, 1970).

Solomons, David, 'The Politicization of Accounting: The Impact of Politics on Accounting Standards', *Journal of Accountancy* (November 1978), pp. 65–72.

Sprouse, Robert T., and Maurice Moonitz, 'A Tentative Set of Broad Accounting Principles for Business Enterprises', *Accounting Research Study No. 3* (New York: AICPA, 1962).

SSAP 15, *Statement of Standard Accounting Practice No. 15: Accounting for Deferred Tax* (revised 1985), (London: Accounting Standards Committee, 1985).

Sterling, Robert R., 'Conservatism: The Fundamental Principle of Valuation in Accounting', *Abacus* (December 1967), pp. 109–32.

Tinker, A., 'Theories of the State and the State of Accounting Economic Reductionism and Political Voluntarism in Accounting Regulation Theory', *Journal of Accounting and Public Policy*, 1984.

Tinker, Tony, *Paper Prophets: A Social Critique of Accounting* (London: Holt, Rinehart & Winston, 1985).

Tomkins, Cyril, and R. A. A. Karim, 'The Shari'ah and Its Implications for Islamic Financial Analysis: An Opportunity to Study Interactions among Society, Organization, and Accounting', *The American Journal of Islamic Social Sciences*, Vol. 4 No. 1 (1987), pp. 101–15.

Whitman, Martin, and Martin Shubik, 'Corporate Reality and Accounting for Investors', *in* S. Zeff and T. Keller (Eds.), *Financial Accounting Theory I* (New York: McGraw-Hill, 1973), pp. 62–72.

Whittington, G., 'Financial Accounting Theory: An Overview', *The British Accounting Review*, Vol. 18 (1986), pp. 4–40.

Zeff, Stephen A., *Forging Accounting Principles in Five Countries: A History and an Analysis of Trends*. Accounting Lectures, 1971. (Champaign, Ill.: Stipes Publishing, 1972).

——, 'The Rise of Economic Consequences', *Journal of Accountancy* (December 1978), pp. 56–63.

Appendix to Chapter 5

I: Islam and Inflation

For the Muslim, the issues raised in the 'changing price-levels' debate single out a number of fundamental questions which cause little concern in the West. Should the currency be *allowed* to fluctuate in general value? Is it perhaps the duty of the State to ensure that the supply of money keeps pace with the volume of transactions being carried out in it? Given the general duty of the Muslim State to maintain conditions in which its citizens can fulfil the requirements of the Shari'a, this might be so. Islam places a great deal of emphasis on the duty to earn one's living by personal effort and involvement. To the extent that inflation permits 'unearned increments', especially at the expense of others, it is an occasion for sin.

Whoever initiates inflation, whether by the issue of banknotes or taking credit, obtains goods and services in return for currency which will buy less in the hands of those who accept it. That said, a Muslim society may be less open to damage by inflation than others. Fixed-interest loans are not permitted, so most lenders will participate in the holding gains of the ventures in which they are concerned. No 'capital-gearing adjustment' could arise. The losses one suffers in inflation are relative to one's uncovered position in monetary assets. Inactive resources of this kind are not looked upon favourably in Islam, although one might feel that their owners should not be made to suffer greater loss than that imposed by the *zakah*.

The question of capital erosion (and so of capital maintenance) is also less acute in a society which frowns upon absentee ownership. Where shareholders have no connection with an enterprise beyond the receipt of dividends and the rarely exercised right to attend general meetings, the question of the realization of reported profit is important. So is the maintenance of the capital at some predetermined level and, hence, some 'ideal' profit. By contrast, people who are more closely aware of the day-to-day management and future plans of their company will be more aware of cash-flow needs. As in a true partnership, they will see the cash they take from the company as 'drawings' against their share of the total equity. Whether those drawings are made against capital or revenue is not significant in the absence of prior agreement to maintain certain capital levels. What is always important is the agreement of all concerned that the drawings are 'fair', as against the common interest.

Nevertheless, Western problems over accounting for changing price-levels are not altogether without relevance to this book as a whole. They illustrate many of the points raised in Chapter 1, such as the ritual nature of money, and the deconstruction of abstract models through common sense. The rational model suggested that changing price-levels would be a major accounting problem, leading to loss of capital base through the overpayment of wages, dividends and taxation. In practice, common sense deconstructed the problem quite effectively. The payment of wages and dividends, and the purchase of capital equipment, are matters of specific policy decisions, and not knee-jerk reactions to profit calculations. As for taxation, governments are well aware of the problem and make arbitrary allowances to cover the problem. In the United Kingdom, for example, a 100 per cent capital allowance was available for the year of purchase, plus a 'stock allowance' to adjust for the unrealized holding gain in the inventories. The US Internal Revenue has permitted the last-in-first-out (LIFO) method of valuing inventory for many years. The *zakah* tax is not a tax on income, so once again 'the bottom line' may in any case be of less significance in Islamic accounting.

A curious feature of the controversy is that economists have consistently preferred to use unadjusted figures of net income in their empirical work (Edwards *et al.*, 1987). This suggests that it is not very useful to attempt a reconciliation between abstract models which have been constructed on differing perceptions of reality.

Bibliography

Edwards, Tereny, John Kay and Colin Mayer, *The Economic Analysis of Accounting Profitability* (Oxford: Clarendon Press, 1987).

Appendix to Chapter 5

II: The Information-Theory Approach to Accounting Theory

In fact, the 'pure' deductive approach to accounting theory, through economic concepts of profit, has not proved very fruitful even for non-Muslims.

In general, the search for true profit foundered, because of the difficulty of reconciling real-life business operations with any existing theory of income. Theoreticians then turned to deducing some accounting theory from the apparent needs of account users. This approach has not enjoyed much greater success, which is our reason for discussing it, for the sake of completeness, in an appendix.

In fact, there is little information about account users and their needs. The studies by Lee and Tweedie (1977, 1981) asked some classes of user how they perceived their own use of these documents. However, no studies to date would appear to have involved actual observation of accounts in use. It is easy to see why this has been so. Few, if any, users of financial statements rely on the single message currently before them as the sole basis for decisions about a company. The financial statements are just one part of the corporate report; that report is just one part of a continuing flow of market-sensitive information put out by the 'investor relations' function of the company's management. Still more information is circulated about the company as part of a more general 'public relations' or 'corporate communications' function. Moreover, a number of agencies outside the control of the company itself will also collect and publish information which is relevant to the company's affairs.

All this heterogeneous information is assembled by its users into a compound interval 'view' of the company; it is this view (*Anschauung*) which is used in making decisions about it. The *Anschauung* will be idiosyncratic to each viewer, depending on how much information has been seen over what period of time, as well as whatever form of information processing may have been used to assemble it. Hence, it is hardly possible to be certain what effect any particular words or figures may have had on a real-life decision. (Laboratory studies tend to use artificial data, so that each subject builds up his or her view exclusively from the given material.) It may be that all that can be hoped for is that any one piece of information will be comprehensible to those to whom it is addressed (Gambling and Beattie, 1986).

It is possible to adopt a contrary 'behaviourist' approach to the use of accounting information. One could enquire as to what measurable changes in behaviour follow from measurable stimuli—under circumstances where a causal relationship may be inferred—without any assumptions about the mental processes involved. The theory of efficient markets is of this type, and it hypothesizes that an efficient market reacts *as if* it had instantaneously compounded all (publicly available) information into its prices.

Studies have demonstrated that many major stock exchanges are of this type; it follows that it is impossible to outperform this market by more informed use of the existing information. Further, other studies have shown that the 'improvements' in available data brought about by the introduction of accounting standards are purely cosmetic. That is to say, they do not seem to add any measurable input to the information before the market. This suggests that the current emphasis among Western standard-setting bodies is mistaken (Beaver, 1981). It would be better to concentrate upon the substance to be disclosed—and whether that substance is in fact comprehensible in the form in which it is presented. The question of the market efficiency of an Islamic Stock Exchange has been discussed in the Appendix to Chapter 4.

These studies of market efficiency have given impetus to the development of a body of theory which seeks to explain the use of information by investment decision-makers. This is 'information economics', which considers information to be a commodity; it follows that there is a market for information, with a demand and a supply. For the first time, this theory recognizes that the retention, preparation and distribution of corporate information is rarely without cost. From this, an agency theory of accounting has been developed: investors demand information, and managers provide it, so long as they find it worthwhile to do so.

These concepts provide some possible insight into the process of setting accounting standards which was discussed earlier in the main body of this chapter. A perfect market for information would require no intervention to produce complete satisfaction. The demand for regulation suggests that this particular market is not perfect. Accordingly, the question of accounting standard-setting is subject to much the same argument as those that apply for and against the regulation of any other market. Perhaps the most notable feature of this argument, for those not accustomed to Western corporate methods, is the proposition that managers are neither employees nor participating capitalists, but essentially independent actors—or agents—whose loyalty to the company and its shareholders is determined by self-interest. The incompatibility of this approach with the Shari'a principles has been discussed in Chapter 4.

Nevertheless, this theory is currently very influential in Western academic accounting theory; it assumes that decision-making involves ranking a finite number of alternative strategies, including strategies of information-gathering, according to their expected pay-offs. The actual pay-off from the decision will depend upon how closely the decision-makers' picture of the situation corresponds with the actual state-of-nature. This state-of-nature is uncertain when the decision has to be taken, but the decision-maker has prior expectations about the probability of various states being the one that actually exists. It is possible, this theory continues, to carry out certain 'experiments' (which usually cost money to perform) which will provide additional information about those prior probabilities. The information may be such that the decision-maker will revise his or her prior probabilities.

The most typical experiment would be taking a sample from a batch of goods. We may have some prior estimate as to how many defective units it contains; as we take larger and larger samples, our uncertainty on this point decreases, until we test the whole batch, and the real state-of-nature is revealed. The theory suggests that we go on increasing the sample until the expected return from improving one's decision is equal to the cost of an additional test.

This marginal approach to information-gathering would not be adequate to define the responsibility of a Muslim decision-maker. We have seen that Muslim business people are not permitted to take an arm's-length view of investment. It is their duty to know what is going on, in an absolute sense, because they are absolutely responsible, before God, for what is done in their name. For example, the concept of 'merchantable quality' might seem to allow for some 'normal' or 'reasonable' level of failure due to partial inspections for faults. However, a Muslim supplier's responsibility for the failure of a product cannot be mitigated by the fact that the batch it was included in had been sampled for inspection to the limit consistent with the price at which it was sold. If the goods have not been subjected to an exhaustive inspection, the buyer should be advised of this, and not left to infer it from its price. This would not be 'fair trading', and so may be a form of *riba*.

Bibliography

Beaver, W. H., *Financial Reporting: An Accounting Revolution* (Englewood Cliffs, N.J.: Prentice-Hall, 1981).

Gambling, T. E., and V. Beattie, 'Effects of the Medium of Communication on the Comprehension and Retention of Messages in Corporate Reports', informal discussion paper (Business School, Portsmouth Polytechnic, January 1986).

Lee, T. A., and D. P. Tweedie, *The Private Shareholders and the Corporate Report* (London: ICAEW, 1977).

—— and ——, *The Institutional Investor and Financial Information* (London: ICAEW, 1981).

Chapter 6

Toward an Islamic Theory of Financial Management

The Responsible Firm

An Islamic Theory of the Firm will have many of the features of Cyert and March's (1963) *A Behavioral Theory of the Firm.* The need for personal responsibility for everything that is done with one's assets precludes any idea of separate corporate goals and policies. However, for the same reason, Muslims would not entertain the proposition that 'collaborators', such as employees, suppliers and customers, were members of the firm—at least on anything approaching the level of the owners. The employees and the others do have an interest in the firm, and we have seen that Islam actually requires them to have a greater concern for it than is common among their non-Muslim counterparts, but they do not and cannot share the responsibility for what is decided. Chapter 2 showed how it is possible for those who contribute nothing but their personal efforts to become responsible for the firm, but this is only by becoming 'officers of the company' and effective partners in the enterprise. In the same way, suppliers and customers could become partners without any tangible investment, but that would be by way of a joint venture.

The interests of the employees and other non-owners whose affairs are affected by the decisions of a firm's owners are clearly safeguarded by the Islamic principles described in Chapter 2. These are primarily those of *adalah* (justice) and *shura* (consultation). There is a duty laid upon all those in any kind of authority to consult with those likely to be affected by proposed changes, and to listen to their views.

The personal responsibility of members for what is done in their names probably leads on to a feature of Muslim business life which may seem odd,

113

even undesirable, to Western eyes. Every individual project undertaken by the company must enjoy a substantial element of personal supervision by every one of those responsible for it. Clearly, this is neither possible nor even desirable in the case of a business of any size, and a wealthy person is likely to have more capital to invest than he or she could properly supervise in this way. This means that very large *continuing* Islamic businesses are only feasible to the extent that some part of their resources can be deployed by way of (Islamic) loans. Islamic lenders take their reward by way of a share of profit and are responsible for what the borrower may do with their money, but this does not involve personal supervision and consultation. The forms which such loans can take have been described at the end of Chapter 2. It might be noted that the Prophet himself traded on his wife's behalf on the basis of a *mudaraba* loan. Of course, these loans can only be used as temporary funding mechanisms, and not as the permanent capital of a company.

It follows that a typical Islamic company might be expected to lie at the centre of a web of joint ventures and consortia. These arrangements are quite common in the West, of course, but usually involve large and sophisticated projects in rather specialized fields of activity. It may be that they will be found to be much more general in Islam. Moreover, it is possible that members of the company will enter into such arrangements with the company itself, whereby they venture some further part of their personal capital in some project, together with a loan from their own company's funds. Although arrangements of this sort are not unknown in the West, they are commonly viewed with some suspicion, since the deals are not 'at arm's length'. However, this may be less of a problem under Islam, where all prices have to be 'fair', whether they are market prices, or even internal transfer prices. The probable existence of a fair number of rather complicated deals of this type means that Islamic companies must be scrupulous in specifying and recording the precise details of all contracts, as will be shown in the next chapter.

This inescapable requirement for personal responsibility and personal consultation probably inhibits the Islamic company from undertaking one major development in corporate organization, which is the occasion of a good deal of controversy between the West, and other, usually less well-developed areas. It is difficult to see how a multinational company could exist under Islam other than in the form of a *mudaraba* loan. Chapter 4 has suggested that partly owned subsidiary companies might be acceptable to Muslims, as a device to permit the local management to exercise the fullest initiative. However, the responsibility of the members of the holding company is in no way diminished. It is important to understand how absolute this responsibility is for Muslims. Owners of resources really do have to look after what is being done with them, and thus cannot spread their interests so far that they cannot keep track of their responsibilities. It is not enough to say 'The buck stops here', or 'On our heads be it'; they actually must know what is going on, and be available to hear the views of those affected by what they do. Present-day facilities for remote electronic conferencing might permit shareholders to reside outside the countries where their assets are deployed, and still conform with the requirements for understanding and consultation. However, the issues discussed in Chapter 1 must cast doubt on the possibility of generating full 'ritual' common sense without more personal contact. At the very least, problems of language and culture would probably inhibit real understanding if the foreign proprietors were not at least fairly frequent visitors to the host country.

Given the central place of the proprietor's personal responsibility under Islam, one must return to the question of what a Muslim is trying to do in life. One must remember that Muslims are 'committed' people, and not 'economic men', pursuing naked self-interest within unusually stringent, but nevertheless external laws of behaviour. Muslims are required to use their assets, including personal skills, to the best advantage. However, since they own those assets as viceregents for God, they are required to seek God's interests rather than their own. This is similar to the position in which medieval canon law sought to place European business people, as described in Chapter 2. Tawney's summary of the latter's view of business activity is similar to the present-day Islamic perspective, in many respects:

> It is right for man to seek such wealth as is necessary for a livelihood in his station. To seek more is not enterprise, but avarice, and avarice is a deadly sin. Trade is legitimate; the different resources of different countries show that it was intended by Providence. But it is a dangerous business. A man must be sure that he carries it on for the public benefit, and that the profits he takes are no more than the wages of his labour. Private property is a necessary institution, at least in a fallen world; men work more and dispute less when goods are private than when they are common. But it is tolerated as a concession to human frailty, not applauded as desirable in itself. (Tawney, 1926, p. 35)

Nevertheless, Islam's view of business is less antagonistic in several important respects. Trade and private property are to be commended, rather than merely tolerated. Property is private because some individual has to take personal responsibility for its use, and accept all the risks and duties attached to it. Moreover, it is not a sin to increase one's wealth as an individual, any more than it is for any other trustees to do so, provided one acquires it fairly and uses it properly. One is simply enhancing the value of the property held in trust as viceregent. This is what is meant by *tazkiyah*. The acceptance of the possibility of social and economic development provides ground for supposing that the Islamic Shari'a may have better prospects of encompassing modern capitalism than did the canon law of medieval Christianity.

As was mentioned in Chapter 2, the Christian Church assumed that agriculture was the natural employment of Man, and hence that 'trade' was at best tolerable, as Tawney says. Like the classical Greek and Roman societies from which these ideas were drawn, the Church did not specify what trade and business consisted of. Islam is quite certain what business is about. It is making and selling goods and services, or trading in such things, either personally, or by personally supervising organizations which do these things. Speculation is strictly forbidden to Muslims. Goods are bought only to be consumed personally or in the course of manufacturing, or to be moved, stored, repackaged, or otherwise improved for resale. Businesses are only to be acquired with a view to running them personally. In short, Islam lays down a clear programme of business morality, and this cuts away many of the difficulties encountered in constructing a theory of financial management. Thus Schall and Haley enquire:

What policies should a firm adopt and what policies would it pursue (in an environment which appears to give a choice between what is moral and what is profitable)? From a moral standpoint there is no generally-acceptable answer, for people differ on what is or is not moral. (Schall and Haley, 1983, p. 7)

Muslims agree on what is or is not moral, and are prohibited from pursuing the profits of immorality.

Western readers might think that this is a policy of moral cowardice. Muslims, it might seem, restrict themselves to small-time, small-town 'hands-on' activity, of the 'Asiatic production' type noted by Marx and Weber. A simple code of morality can cover all eventualities. We have argued, in Chapter 4, that methods of organization could be found which permitted the deployment of very large sums of capital without infringing the requirements of the Shari'a. The problem is over what 'business sin' actually consists of. Simple oppressive dealing is only part of the sin; in Muslim eyes, it is equally wrong to 'play games' with the wealth which is held in trust for God, by treating other people and their livelihoods as counters on a Monopoly board.

Islamic Finance

If all business that is permissible for Muslims is also morally desirable, it follows that the goals of Muslim management do not differ from those of Western management: namely, the maximization of the value of the enterprise. The fact that the Muslim proprietor is seen as a trustee makes no difference to the objective as such, but only to the distribution of any surplus as dividends, or their re-investment as retained earnings. Of course, 'the value of the business' which is to be maximized is likely to be very different in the case of an Islamic firm. The concept of return on investment (ROI) is not acceptable. Not only does it imply that money has a time value, but it also requires assumptions about the future which are both impious and most unlikely to be correct! Once again, we can see the essential pragmatism of Islam: Muslims are not interested in extrapolations of the past into the future. Their concern is to put their talents and assets to work, to best advantage, in the foreseeable future.

Here, 'to best advantage' means 'so as to secure the optimum cash-flow in the period under review'. This method of ranking economic opportunities has been observed among other peoples who, for one reason or another, do not recognize ROI. We have argued in Chapter 1, and elsewhere (Gambling, 1987), that such a criterion does not necessarily evidence a lack of economic sophistication. The ROI approach requires both the existence of financial markets, and a faith in their operations validity. The optimum cash-flow for an Islamic enterprise is that which maximizes the value of the business, when taken together with the closing value of the firm's assets. Chapter 5 suggested that the ideal Islamic valuation might be net realizable value, along the Continuously Contemporary Accounting (CoCoA) lines proposed by Chambers. There is a problem here, in so far as this approach is used for forward planning. It would be necessary to consider what the future CoCoA values of the various items might be. The concept is probably anathema to Chambers himself, whose principal argument was for the removal of all elements of estimation of the future from accounting! At the pragmatic level, this difficulty suggests another reason why a Muslim's time horizon should be rather short.

Given a disinclination to foretell the future, one's planning time horizon is nothing more than that period during which it is feasible to make detailed plans of what to make, buy and sell, given the personnel, plant and demand likely to be available. This means that Muslim business people might be expected to base their decisions upon a medium-range financial plan, for no more than a few months ahead, with a maximum period of about twelve months. This 'short-sighted' approach may have much to commend it. The success of many Japanese businesses can be attributed to a policy of continual innovation. This involves an annual, year-long exercise to design and develop 'next year's products'. At the same time, the company formulates a plan to make and sell those products in the ensuing twelve months (Tsuchiya, 1987). Clearly, this form of planning is another feature of the 'world-class manufacturing' techniques to which we have already referred more than once. A plan of this sort is a necessary support for the long-term relationships with suppliers and customers, which make 'Just In Time' inventory control possible. It also underlies the stable personnel policies and 'quality circle' consultations which are as much a part of the Muslim business culture as they are of the Japanese business culture.

A similar pragmatism underlies the Muslim approach to long-range planning. In a general way, global, conglomerate business expansion must so attenuate the personal responsibility of those who undertake it as to be unacceptable in Islam. As a result, Muslim business people may be less concerned with such abstractions as 'corporate mission', or the proposition that some toe-hold in another industry suggests a policy of forward or backward integration into another line of business. The question for Muslims is more likely to concern 'what needs to be set in hand now, for delivery and commissioning at some date beyond the medium-range planning period'—in the light of what the decision-makers currently feel themselves called to do. This reflects the fact that Muslims do not believe that Man can create his own future.

It can be seen that Muslim financial management is a straightforward exercise in budgeting, in which the issues discussed in Western work on 'finance' play no part. 'There is no finance in corporate financial models' (Brealey and Myers, 1981, p. 645). This serves to emphasize the ephemeral nature of Western financial theory. Market prices have no history, and hence they do not have a future either. Like much econometric work, the theory provides rich and insightful explanations of the present position, but little guide as to future positions. Since Muslim investors have to manage businesses rather than 'portfolios of investments', they are compelled to take thought of the practicalities of corporate planning.

Given this approach to corporate finance, the 'cost of capital' is literally whatever has to be paid out to the providers of capital during the budget period, whether by way of a share of profit, or repayment of capital. The capital-budgeting exercise reduces to a consideration of how contracted payments, of whatever nature, are going to affect the cash-flow position, as defined. In this respect it will breach the Western convention that the specific method used to finance an acquisition is not relevant to the investment decision, except in so far as it affects the overall cost of capital of the enterprise. The concept of an overall cost of capital is virtually meaningless in an Islamic context. Indeed, since Islamic borrowing involves a sharing of profits and losses, a major consideration may be over how the cash-flow can be partitioned equitably, in circumstances where the loan relates to some specific project(s), as opposed to providing general finance for the whole undertaking.

In any case, financial analysis is only one element in a Muslim capital budget. The real criterion is a depth of conviction that the investment is the right thing to do. As we have seen, the *al-Istikhara* prayer shows that this aspect of decision-making is well founded in the Shari'a; at the same time, the prayer is an acknowledgement of God's omnipotence rather than a fortune-teller's incantation. Muslim business people say the prayer—but still have to decide what to do. The difference in their approach will be that such decisions are most likely to be couched in non-financial terms: the future of some technology, the reliability of some source of supply, or the expected strength of some market. It is unlikely that they will seek to back up those convictions by extrapolating estimates of cash-flows far beyond the period covered by their regular budgets.

As has been seen in Chapter 5, the traditional Western discounted cash-flow computation makes strong assumptions about the availability of further investments in the future which often cannot be justified in the real world. What this means for the Muslim business is that choices between competing schemes for long-term capital investments have to be founded on judgements about their technical and commercial merits, without 'working the oracle' through largely untestable propositions about future cash-flows (Gambling, 1977). It could be argued (from what was said in Chapter 1) that the preparation of the traditional 'capital project appraisal', using discounted cash-flow computations, was a typical ritual use of accounting. It may be that this is the effect of the calculations in Western decision-making. On the other hand, we have emphasized that the proliferation of ritual is never desirable; a straightforward debate over the merits of the proposals is adequate to deconstruct whatever models are used to advance them.

Project Analysis under Islam

The reason why Muslim business people can adopt a policy of maximizing cash-flow may need further explanation. The Shari'a requires 'just wages' to be paid, and 'just prices' to be charged. The just wage is whatever is necessary to maintain the worker in an appropriate station of life, including the ability to support dependants, and meet the liability to *zakah*. The just price is whatever is necessary to cover the expected average cost of production and distribution, including just wages to employees, just prices to suppliers, and a just reward to the proprietors.

This average assumes a normal demand, normal efficiency of operation, and normal levels of plant utilization. Super-profits, or losses, become available to the proprietors as sales, efficiency and plant-utilization vary from the norm, and drive the actual average cost below or above the fair price. In so far as the calculation of a just price involves estimates of these norms, it is a subjective procedure, akin to budgeting in the general way. Agency theory would suggest that those concerned would have an incentive to 'pad their budgets', so as to ensure a safe margin of super-profit. The assumption must be that Muslims possess a degree of commitment to Islam which would inhibit such deception. Moreover, the purpose of institutions such as the Religious Supervisory Boards (mentioned in Chapter 4 and elsewhere) and the office of *hisbah* (mentioned in Chapter 3) would be to examine the *bona fides* of this type of calculation.

An Islamic business which cannot produce super-profits will show a nil return on capital, after paying its proprietors their just reward, net of any actual losses incurred. Muslim investors may be expected to move their capital into areas where they believe super-profits may be found, subject to the need to limit their search to areas where they can provide a responsible managerial input. Where no super-profits can be found, Muslim investors will still utilize their capital, as long as any resulting loss does not exceed the amount of the additional *zakah* payable on uninvested funds. It may be a moot point whether Muslims may sell below the fair price, either to keep their plant running, or to gain entry for a product into a market. Intent must be everything. Short-term arrangements to tide over a slack period, or introduce a new product to a new market may be acceptable. It would not be legitimate, say, to have a long-term policy of dumping goods on overseas markets below cost, while maintaining tariffs to 'protect' the home market from re-importations!

Let us turn to some examples of how the Islamic cash-flow approach to investment appraisal would work Initially, we will assume that unlimited amounts of capital can be invested in any project, in multiples of the appropriate project/unit:

Project	Investment per unit (%)	ROI (%)	Net cash-flow per unit, before managerial reward (%)
A	1,250	40	500
B	10,000	25	2,500
C	50,000	12	6,000
D	100,000	8	8,000

If one had $1m to invest, one would achieve the 'correct' (ROI) ordering of the projects on the cash-flow figures:

Project	No. of units bought for $1m	Total net cash-flow ($)	Preference order
A	800	400,000	1st
B	100	250,000	2nd
C	20	120,000	3rd
D	10	80,000	4th

One should invest up to the maximum amount which could be invested in each project, in that order. For non-Muslims, it is obvious that the cash-flows are simply the product of the ROI and the capital sum invested! However, this statement is less naive than it might seem, in an Islamic setting. The cash flows are calculated before charging anything for managerial reward. An acceptable project can only be one that charges fair prices, so these net cash-flows will be no more than fair compensation for the managerial effort and entrepreneurial judgement of risk required by the project. The significance of the ranking is therefore rather different for Muslims: Project A represents the best use of the investor's trust from God, in resources *and talent*.

Where the numbers of available units do not permit the full expenditure of the whole amount to be invested in the first-ranking project, or the unit cost of an investment is not a factor of the total amount available, the decision may be more complex, involving mathematical programming, much as is done in similar circumstances outside 'Islam (Weingartner, 1963). A further complication may be that certain projects are mutually exclusive for some reason. Again, since the objective is always to maximize the cash flow, the 'Western' and 'Islamic' solutions will be identical, assuming that the Western and Islamic calculations of the amount of the cash-flows are the same.

These programming techniques always abandon the naive ROI ranking, and rank projects by their ability to generate cash-flow. In the very simple example set out above, the two rankings are identical because there are no limitations on the selection of the investments. In practice, a Muslim's opportunities for investment are likely to be severely limited, in one direction at least. He or she has to undertake a degree of personal involvement in the management, and it is not unusual for projects requiring a low investment of capital to require as much or even more input from the proprietor than a larger project. If one assumed that each project-unit required the full-time attention of its owner, the example given above would have a solution which completely reversed the naive ROI order of preference. Provided one has at least $100,000 to invest, it is better to invest in a unit of Project D (and receive $8,000) than to invest in Project A (and receive only $500), or B and C either. It is better to obtain a low return on capital and live well than starve on a very good return on capital. A practical example of this dilemma is described by Acheson (1972).

The problems facing Muslims over ranking investments is likely to be further complicated by the fact that, although one has to involve oneself personally in their operations, some partners may be more active in day-to-day supervision than others. The degree to which this is done is reflected in the relative shares of profits and losses agreed between the parties. In particular, it will be remembered that loans from Islamic banks will typically involve such an arrangement. Suppose that the various degrees of involvement in the projects in the example given above resulted in the following profit-sharing arrangements between Partner X (who contributes only personal service) and Partner Y (who provides the whole of the capital). There are no restrictions on the amounts which can be invested in any one project:

Project	Partner X's share (%)	Partner Y's share (%)	Y's share of total cash-flow ($)	Y's naive order of preference
A	90	10	40,000	4th
B	70	30	187,500	1st
C	30	70	84,000	2nd
D	10	90	72,000	3rd

Y's preference is 'naive' because we do not know how much of his or her time would be absorbed by the various projects, or whether Y has other projects, perhaps including an existing business, which also need attention. The solution will be a 'Weingartner' exercise which will find the mixture of projects that will absorb the partners' time and resources to best advantage overall.

Islam and Business Risk

Given the Muslim concern for the strict morality of insurance contracts, mentioned in Chapter 4, Muslim business people may be expected to give considerable thought to the risks involved in what they plan to do. Neither fatalism nor the sort of 'confidence' which leads some Christian fundamentalists to pick up rattlesnakes has any part in Islam. The Muslims' disinclination to foresee the future as an extrapolation of the past may make them unusually conscious of the downside of any investment proposal. It may fail to generate any positive cash-flow, while leaving the owners' commitments to be met in full. Chapter 3 says something of the Islamic approach to insolvency. Creditors are required to be merciful to those who cannot pay on the due date, and families are charged with the duty of helping out members in financial difficulties; however, there is no way in which a debt can be 'discharged', otherwise than by payment in full, by someone, at some time. A Muslim cannot trade on credit without a specific 'worst case' plan for meeting his or her debts.

In any case, adherence to the basic Shari'a principles is likely to enhance one's sensitivity to the risks inherent in any course of action. Niemark and Tinker (1986) cite instances where the policy decisions of managements have proved counter-productive, in the crassest of economizing senses, because they have overlooked the interactions between the corporation and its environment over the longer period. It might seem a useful move for a large multinational corporation to destabilize an unfriendly government, for example. However, this has commonly proved a most unprofitable strategy in practice, since subsequent, more amenable, governments often seem to lack the stability of the original! Islamic insistence upon legitimate succession, election and loyalty (noted in Chapter 2) would forbid an attempt to destabilize a legitimate government, in any case. More generally, the insistence upon the principles of *khilafa* and *shura* should make Islamic companies aware of 'common-sense' externalities of all kinds. Muslim decision-makers should have a much richer common-sense intuition of the likely outcomes of anything they might consider doing.

Muslims are not permitted to gamble, in business matters or otherwise. Thus, an investor facing the facts set out in the example given above would be expected to undertake some sensitivity analysis that took account of the relative riskiness of projects. Supposing the cash-flows in the example are 'the most likely case', there might be, say, a 10 per cent probability that the return from Project A might be less than $100 per unit. If there was only a 10 per cent chance that the return from Project B would be less than $2,000 per unit, a single investment of $1m in A has a 10 per cent chance of producing only $80,000 or less, while the same investment in B has the same chance for $200,000 or less. Other things being equal, the better downside probability of Project B would suggest some mixture of investments in the two projects (and maybe all four), notwithstanding the overall superiority of Project A, on average.

In practice, the mixture of investments in a portfolio should depend not only upon the probabilities of the returns, but also on the correlations between them. Project B would become more desirable, the less its return tended to vary in sympathy with that of Project A. The mathematics of this type of problem have been well explored in recent years (see Brealey and Myers, 1981, Chapter 7). Diversification will largely eliminate the 'unique risk' of the various projects, but the 'market risk', or its more specific equivalent within a firm, cannot be avoided. A non-Muslim investor can select a portfolio which contains whatever element of unique risk appeals to his or her risk preference. Since a Muslim is viceregent of the resources to be invested, it can be seen that he or she should set aside personal timidity or rashness, as far as is possible, and act as any other trustee ought to do in the same circumstances. In fact, a very limited diversification over six or seven investments seems to suffice to remove a high proportion of the unique risk from a portfolio. One might suppose that the Muslim investor ought always to diversify to that extent, but not seek excessive security beyond that point. Prudent risk-taking is actually required of 'the good steward'.

Risk and the Islamic Company

Much of what has been said in the preceding sections has been in terms of investments made by Muslim business people out of their own private resources. This was an appropriate approach, since, as we said at the beginning of the chapter, an Islamic company can have no aims or policies beyond those of its members. Nevertheless, an Islamic company can and will accumulate resources 'of its own', unless these are actually distributed to its members. In a general way, it is likely that the members of the firm will use those resources directly, both for current trading and the purchase of fixed assets, rather than distribute them and then solicit their return. Certainly, issues of 'corporate leverage', 'dividend policy' and 'retention of earnings' have an extensive coverage in conventional Western financial theory.

For example, it is sometimes claimed that enterprises ought not to attempt to adjust the risks of investing their stock, because the individual shareholder can always adjust his or her portfolio to suit their personal preference. Western companies can do this quite directly in the form of leverage, by issuing fixed-interest securities. Muslim loans can never bear a fixed interest. However, the likelihood that the lender's share of profit may be rather low (because of minimal personal intervention), and a larger proportion, if not all, of any losses may be borne by the lender, will have some effect on the risk attaching to the long-term equity in an Islamic company.

The proof (and disproof) of the proposition that leverage is a matter of indifference in a perfect capital market is complicated by the probability that no market is absolutely perfect. There may well be unsatisfied investors looking for a type of security which cannot be built up through diversifying their portfolios (Brealey and Myers, 1981, Chapter 17). As we have suggested in the Appendix to Chapter 4, an Islamic capital market is likely to be less than perfect, in the technical sense. The need for personal involvement in one's investments must limit the degree of *external* diversification which can be achieved. At the same time, the Muslim investor's 'insider' status should enable him or her to influence the *internal* diversification of risk quite directly.

Rather similar considerations apply to dividend policies (Brealey and Myers, 1981, Chapter 16). In a perfect capital market, it would make no difference whether earnings are distributed or retained. Those who want to save can invest their dividends, while those who want to spend could sell part of their (enhanced) shareholding. The issue can be complicated to the extent that corporate dividends are taxed differently (usually more heavily) from earnings retained within the company. Moreover, dividends are commonly more heavily taxed than 'capital gains' on the sale of shares whose market value has been enhanced by internally financed growth. For Muslims, the *zakah* tax should be the same wherever the assets and income are to be found, but this need not be true of taxes raised for non-religious purposes.

The evidence suggests that Western investors commonly do respond to 'dividend policy' to some extent, perhaps because they see a steady but not excessive pay-out of cash as evidence that the company is not hard-pressed for cash (on the one hand), or short of opportunities for investment (on the other). It seems probable that Muslim investors' necessarily closer involvement with the management of the company would reduce their reliance on evidence of this type.

Although Muslims may have the knowledge needed to influence the internal financing and investment decisions of their companies, one might wonder whether they will always have the political power necessary to achieve their personally desired levels of income, growth and risk. Arrow's Impossibility Theorem might suggest that a Pareto-optimal solution cannot exist to problems of this type, in the absence of dictatorship! However, consultation is the name of the game in Islamic management, so the individual shareholder should have ample opportunity for discussing these issues. Since one's fellow-shareholders are trustees of their wealth, they have a duty to give proper consideration to the arguments of others, and decide issues with reference to Shari'a principles, rather than naked self-interest. Arrow's Theorem, like the rest of economic theory, cannot be applied to the actions of committed people (Sen, 1976–7). It would follow that real points of difference ought to be slight, and confined largely to *a priori* judgements as to the likely outcomes of investments.

Some Specifically 'Islamic' Problems of Corporate Finance

The fact that the Muslim shareholder has something of the status of a partner will produce some difficulties which are not met with among their Western counterparts. If a Western shareholder disapproves of management decisions, the simple solution is to dispose of the shares and buy others in companies whose policies appear more congenial. Indeed, Western shareholders may not be much concerned with the nature of the decisions being taken in their name; their interest is in the reaction of the market toward the company. By contrast, the Muslim shareholder is more 'locked into' the investment, but is entitled to say, 'If you gave me my share of the money as a dividend, I could do better elsewhere'—and be listened to.

The arguments ranged against the request for a dividend might be the indivisible nature of the proposed internal investment, or the proposition that the internal investment was vital to the continued existence of the company. The solution might be simple. The dividend could be set at a rate acceptable to the dissenting shareholders; the other members could re-invest the excess part of their dividend in the company, while the dissenter's portion could be made good by borrowing. The costs of servicing the loan would have to be met out of future profits, so their share of those costs would fall upon the dissenters. Given a perfect capital market, it would be as if they had borrowed the money themselves to finance their preferred private schemes. Of course, the effect of taxation and the admitted imperfections of the capital market might prevent so neat a solution to the disagreement. Then some other accommodation would have to be reached.

The question of maintaining the viability of the firm could be more serious. Since loans are not fixed-interest bearing, but joint ventures in future profits, it is unlikely that any loan could be raised by a company that was not doing very well. In short, it is conceivable that the reason the shareholder could invest to better advantage outside the company is simply that the company is failing. Now a Western shareholder is entitled to sell the shares for what they will fetch, and forget the matter. However, a Muslim investor has to bear the responsibilities of the investment, as well as its benefits. Accordingly, if the company is failing, he or she ought to do something about it, for the sake of society as a whole. Ideally, this will involve reviving the company in some way, but if that is not possible, the shareholders must pursue the orderly winding-up of its activities.

Shareholders cannot take dividends while a company is unable to meet its debts as they fall due, either under Islam or in the West. However, the restrictions on dividend payments in an Islamic company may go beyond technical insolvency. Provided always that the creditors can be paid in full, it may be the duty of Muslim shareholders to carry on trading at the cost of further losses of capital, in order to do justice to the claims of the other 'collaborators' in the firm, such as employees, suppliers and customers. It follows that further capital projects may have to be undertaken whose return is totally unattractive; there is a duty to apply internal funds to this purpose, if they are available.

Moreover, the link between the availability of a share of profit and the appropriateness of paying it out as a dividend is less strong under Islam than in the West. Muslims are expected to earn enough to maintain them-selves and their dependants in an appropriate condition of life. They are also expected to seek to earn surpluses, but as trustees of their own talents and assets. Thus, a shareholder whose share of profit is surplus to his or her needs had better have a good purpose for the surplus, if only to distribute it as charitable donations in excess of the normal liability to *zakah*. Conversely, a wealthy shareholder ought to consider the necessity of poorer shareholders, and be prepared to give away surplus income so that others can have a reasonable income from their shareholdings.

Islamic financial management seeks to harness the natural human drives to create surpluses, and measure them in terms of money, which were noted in Chapter 1. Its purpose is to divert those drives both from the modern self-interest of the economizing spirit, and from the earlier use of such surpluses, as wasteful offerings to deities and the like. At the same time, it is essential not to blunt these drives, because they are the mainspring of civilized human development. All this is to be achieved, it is hoped, by emphasizing Man's viceregency of his own assets and talents. Both must be utilized to the full, neither for self-aggrandisement nor for superstitious expenditures, but for socially responsible developments which are pleasing to God, because they conform to God's laws.

Bibliography

Acheson, J. M., 'Accounting Concepts and Economic Opportunities in a Tarascan Village: Emic and Etic Views', *Human Organization*, Vol. 31 (1972), pp. 83–91.

Brealey, Richard, and Stewart Myers, *Principles of Corporate Finance* (New York: McGraw-Hill, 1981).

Cyert, R. M., and J. G. March, *A Behavioral Theory of the Firm* (Englewood Cliffs, N.J.: Prentice-Hall, 1963).

Gambling, Trevor, 'Magic, Accounting and Morale', *Accounting, Organizations and Society*, Vol. 2 (1977), pp. 141–51.

——, 'Accounting for Rituals', *Accounting, Organizations and Society*, Vol. 12 (1987), pp. 319–29.

Neimark, M., and T. Tinker, 'The Social Construction of Management Control Systems', *Accounting, Organizations and Society*, Vol. 11 (1986), pp. 369–95.

Schall, I. D., and C. W. Haley, *Introduction to Financial Management*, 3rd Edition (New York: McGraw-Hill, 1983).

Sen, A. K., 'Rational Fools: A Critique of the Behavioural Foundations of Economic Theory', *Philosophy and Public Affairs*, Vol. 6 (1976–7), pp. 317–44.

Tawney, R. H., *Religion and the Rise of Capitalism: An Historical Study* (London: Murray, 1926).

Tsuchiya, M., 'The Growth Strategies of Japanese Companies: In Search of Excellence', *Economia Aziendale*, Vol. VI (1987), pp. 59–77.

Weingartner, H. Martin, *Mathematical Programming and the Analysis of Capital Budgeting Problems* (Englewood Cliffs, N.J.: Prentice-Hall, 1963).

Appendix to Chapter 6

The Anwar Automobile Group of Companies: A Case Study

Note: This case study suggests how the Shari'a principles (as interpreted in this text) might be applied to a group of companies. It may be that the principles are already applied less formally in many Muslim enterprises. For example, we show how the shares of profits might be built up from basic facts about the members' various contributions to the company. Such shares are commonly negotiated rather than calculated; however, the negotiations would have to take informal account of the facts as stated.

The Anwar Automobile Group is a newly established group of Islamic companies. It manufactures a single homogeneous product, the 'Anwar' saloon car. The structure of the company is a holding company, Anwar Holding, which deals with finance and marketing for the group, and Anwar Alpha and Anwar Beta, which operate two manufacturing plants. The Group is linked through common shareholders and directors, and by the intention of all the shareholders that each company should follow common policies.

Since these are Islamic companies, all the members are expected to take some part in the management of their companies, and receive a fair wage for their services, in addition to their reward as entrepreneurs, for investing and risking their capital in the venture. However, the sole rewards of membership are by way of shares of profit, because of the objection to any member being rewarded by way of a lump sum. Unlike 'salaried partners' in Western firms, the members' rewards for services should not be taken from profits in priority to other rewards, but amalgamated into the overall share of profit.

In this example, it is assumed that only three classes of skill are to be found among the members: engineers (F and I), who should receive $50,000 a year for full-time working; professionals (A to E), who should get $40,000; and technicians (G to K), who get $20,000. It is also assumed that the rewards for entrepreneurship in this instance should be $10,000 per $100,000 invested. The (%) figure represents the percentage of the members' time devoted to the company. The ratios for distributing profits and losses are calculated by compounding the relative 'rewards for risk-taking' and 'rewards for services' as in Table 1.

The total capital of $5½m subscribed by the members is invested in the appropriate undertakings. We have argued, in the main text, that the assets in an Islamic company will always be valued as for *zakah* purposes. It was also suggested that Chambers' Continuously Contemporary Accounting (CoCoA) would provide a suitable basis for this. There is a problem here: some very costly items, of vital importance to the company, have no CoCoA value at all. In general, this correctly reflects the resources potentially available for redeployment (including the payment of *zakah*). Where a company has many such 'non-vendible' durable assets, the effect would be to show substantial losses, especially in the early years of a company's life. Again, this fairly reflects the situation for that purpose. However, we need to consider the more gradual amortization of these assets in arriving at a fair price for the company's goods and services. Let us suppose that the initial capital is invested as set out in Table 2.

It is now possible to calculate the initial 'fair price' of the 'Anwar' saloon. Assume that 200 cars will be made during the first year; 100 in each plant. Also assume that the fixed assets all have an expected life of five years, with no residual value. It is necessary to calculate normal historical-cost amortization for *both* types of fixed asset *in these calculations*. It is hardly possible to estimate future CoCoA values. In fact, to attempt to do so would be anathema to Islam—and to Professor Chambers! However, the only reason the amortization charge used in the following calculation is based on the historical cost *of the assets actually in use* is that this is the first year of operation. One must suppose (since these are Islamic companies pursuing *tazkiyah*) that the assets acquired are those which will enable the 'Anwar' saloon to be made most effectively. How this amortization would be calculated in subsequent periods will be discussed later in the case. The fair price is always based upon some fair use of the most effective plant, as in Table 3.

The fair price of the car is therefore $25,000. Because this price is fair, this

Table 1   *Ratios for distribution of profits and losses*

Members	Investment	Reward for risk-taking	Reward for services			Share of profit	loss
	($k)	*($k)*	*($k)*	*(%)*	*(= $k due)*		
Anwar Holding Company							
A	100	10	40	50	20	3/15	3/15
B	100	10	40	50	20	3/15	3/15
C	100	10	40	50	20	3/15	3/15
D	100	10	40	50	20	3/15	3/15
E	100	10	40	50	20	3/15	3/15
		$50			$100		
Anwar Alpha Company							
A	100	10	40	50	20	3/35	1/25
B	100	10	40	50	20	3/35	1/25
F	0	0	50	100	50	5/35	0
G	1,100	110	20	25	5	11½/35	11/25
H	1,200	120	20	25	5	12½/35	12/25
		$250			$100		
Anwar Beta Company							
C	100	10	40	50	20	3/35	1/25
D	100	10	40	50	20	3/35	1/25
I	0	0	50	100	50	5/35	10
J	1,500	150	20	25	5	15½/35	15/25
K	800	80	20	25	5	8½/35	8/25
		$250			$100		

Notes

1. F and I are members of their respective companies, although they contribute nothing apart from 100 per cent of their services; they are entitled to a share of any profit, but they do not share in any losses, which are chargeable against capital only.

2. Obviously, the entrepreneurs' rewards can be calculated only after the end of the trading period. Any drawings made during the period would be by way of an advance against expected profits, and shown as members' current accounts with the companies.

3. A, B, C and D are members of both the Holding Company and Alpha Company or Beta Company. It is these cross-holdings which link the companies into a 'group'.

Table 2   *Investment of initial capital*

	Anwar Holding Company ($k)	Anwar Alpha Company ($k)	Anwar Beta Company ($k)
'Non-vendible' fixed assets	100	800	800
'Vendible' fixed assets	300	1,000	1,000
Working capital	100	700	700

The Alpha and Beta plants are, initially, identical.

Table 3   *Calculation of the 'fair price'*

	($k)	Anwar Saloon ($k)	Services of Anwar Holding Company ($k)
Members' remuneration for risk-taking		550	50
Members' remuneration for services		300	100
Amortization of 'non-vendible' fixed assets		340	20
Amortization of 'vendible' fixed assets		460	60
Estimated 'fair' operating costs:			
Anwar Holding Company	270		270
Anwar Alpha Company	1,540		
Anwar Beta Company	1,540	3,350	
		$5,000	$500

is the price at which the Anwar Companies will market the car. The fact that its nearest rival sells locally at $30,000 is no reason, to a Muslim, why the car should be sold at (say) $29,000. The fair price of the services of Anwar Holding Company to the subsidiaries is $250,000 each.

Let us assume that the Anwar Group of Companies actually succeeds in making 200 cars, and selling them for $25,000 each. The cash-flows of the companies might be as in Table 4.

The fact that the Anwar Group of Companies are Islamic companies

Table 4   *Calculation of cash-flows*

	($k)	Anwar Holding Company ($k)	($k)	Anwar Alpha Company ($k)	($k)	Anwar Beta Company ($k)
Sales				2,500		2,500
Transfer price of services		(500)	250		250	
Operating costs		270	1,500	1,750	1,560	1,180
'Operating cash-flow'		230		750		690
Expenditure on fixed assets:						
'Non-vendible'	20		180		150	
'Vendible '	60	80	205	385	195	345
'Overall cash-flow'		$150		$365		$345

complicates the question of ascertaining their 'net income'. The prices they have charged are just prices, and the members are entitled to their just rewards. These are calculated without direct reference to actual perform- ance, as we have demonstrated. The question of whether the members are entitled to draw their just rewards, or even more than their just reward, depends upon (a) the efficiency with which they have operated the plant, and (b) *the efficiency and justice with which they have maintained the capital of the group.* We shall argue that (b) involves more specific issues than can be covered by the Western-style charge for amortization. Bearing in mind the need to adjust values to CoCoA wherever possible, it might be possible to extend the calculation of cash-flow as in Table 5.

We would argue that these surpluses and deficits have some claim (but not an absolute claim) to be the true income of an Islamic company. It is necessary to consider the analysis of how the surplus/(deficit) items are made up (Table 6). The 'CoCoA adjustments' are unrealized profits or losses; the profits are not available for dividend. The 'Operating efficiency variances' are realized surpluses or deficits, calculated with reference to the 'fair operating costs' used in calculating the fair prices. These are available for dividend, if positive, provided that they reflect true economy, *and not simple underspending on items which should have been incurred.*

The 'Under/(Over)spending on fixed assets' is the difference between the

Table 5 *Calculation of cash-flow (adjusted)*

	Anwar Holding Company ($k)	Anwar Alpha Company ($k)	Anwar Beta Company ($k)
Overall cash-flow	150	365	345
Add 'CoCoA adjustment'[1]	5	50	(12)
Funds available to members	155	415	333
Less Fair reward to members	150	350	350
Surplus/(Deficit)	$5	$65	$(17)

Table 6 *Analysis of surplus/(deficit)*

	Anwar Holding Company ($k)	Anwar Alpha Company ($k)	Anwar Beta Company ($k)
'CoCoA adjustment'	5	50	(12)
Operating efficiency variance	0	40	(2)
Under/(Over)spending on fixed assets	0	(25)	15
	$5	$65	$(17)

allowance for amortization included in the calculation of the fair prices, and what was actually spent in the period. The items represent an application of their surplus by the members of Anwar Alpha Company, and a retrenchment by the members of Anwar Beta Company. Such discrepancies between charges for amortization and expenditure on assets are never considered in arriving at Western-style corporate income. The reason is that the Western charges for amortization are seen as a provision for the future replacement of assets currently in use; as such, they have no relevance to expenditure during the period. As usual, the Islamic company takes a more pragmatic view: the assets are almost never truly replaced. That is why, subsequent to the first budget-period, calculations of fair prices will *not* use the historical-cost depreciation of assets actually in use. Instead, they will consider what *would* be the amortization on an ideal, state-of-the-art plant, capable of manufacturing a (possibly improved) Anwar Saloon at maximum efficiency. The operating costs will also relate to that ideal plant.

This 'idealistic' approach is justified by the Muslim objective of *tazkiyah*. The 'total quality commitment' of 'world-class manufacturing' is central to Islamic manufacturing. It is the duty of the members of the group to bring their plant into line with best practice *at all times*. If this actually costs more or less than the allowance included in the fair price operating for the period, that is one of the trading risks for which they are being rewarded to undertake. Good management involves so planning the repair and overhaul of plant, as well as its retirement and purchase, that the overall cost is kept to a minimum.

The real problem is one of smoothing the income of the companies. It might seem that if comparatively little is spent in one year, this is likely to be made up in later years. Obviously, it is possible, even likely, that Anwar Beta Company has not bought all the fixed assets needed to achieve state-of-the-art efficiency in the coming year. The Muslim answer would be that this is managerial misfeasance; if it could be bought now, then it ought to be bought now. Carrying forward a provision to do so is no substitute for right action. In fact, the Muslim business person's duty to maintain capital is to do so in real terms, and at all times. This is why we claimed, in Chapters 3 and 5, that 'accounting for changing price levels' is a non-problem in Islam. It is only funds which are retained in monetary assets that are reduced by inflation—as they are also reduced by *zakah*!

The effect of this approach to accounting is apparent from the balance sheets of the companies (Table 7).

Note

1. It is assumed that the working capital is constant and that its CoCoA value does not change over the period. The CoCoA adjustment is in respect of CoCoA-valuable fixed assets only, and is the net of holding gains and holding losses, additions and wear-and-tear. The calculation is simply:

	Anwar Holding Company ($k)	Anwar Alpha Company ($k)	Anwar Beta Company ($k)
Initial purchase	300	1,000	1,000
Current CoCoA valuation	305	1,050	988
CoCoA adjustment	$5	$50	$(12)

Table 7 *Balance sheets of the three hypothetical companies*

	Anwar Holding Company ($k)	Anwar Alpha Company ($k)	Anwar Beta Company ($k)
Net Assets			
Working capital	100	700	700
Cash ('Overall cash-flow')	150	365	345
Fixed assets at CoCoA valuation	305	1,050	988
	$555	$2,115	$2,033
Net Member's Equity			
Capital subscribed	500	2,500	2,500
Less Initial investment in non-vendible assets	100	800	800
	400	1,700	1,700
Add Retained earnings ('Funds available to members')	155	415	333
	$555	$2,115	$2,033

Notes
1. No drawings against profits have been made by the members.
2. The original capital is shown reduced by the initial investment in non-vendible assets. This could be interpreted along the same lines as in the old 'double account system' formerly used by British railway companies: Islamic companies have a duty to maintain their basic undertaking in perfect, state-of-the-art condition at all times *as a charge against current income.*

Chapter 7

Toward an Islamic Theory of Corporate Information

The Managerial Basis of Islamic Accounting

Although more than a thousand years have passed since the death of the Prophet, what we have written in the preceding chapters shows that Islam has a direct and detailed message about the ownership and management of modern businesses. Moreover, the message is positive, even for the largest and most intricate of organizations, and we believe that the Shari'a principles can be applied without difficulty to any modern business undertaking. This may be all the easier because of the historical difficulties, described in the Appendix to Chapter 2, which have prevented the development of large-scale capitalist enterprise in Muslim countries, otherwise than on Western lines. There is very little by way of pre-existent Islamic theory or practice requiring reform or replacement to accommodate recent social or technological innovations.

This may be especially true of Islamic accounting theory. The Muslim investor is bound to be concerned over what the enterprise is doing, even if some other people are dealing with its day-to-day operation. Moreover, the concern of the State, and the community at large, is also centred upon the way in which the business is being run. There can be no class of *rentiers*, for whom non-specialist 'financial accounts' need to be prepared; Islamic accounting is always managerial accounting. Islamic accounting theory will be a theory of managerial accounting. Such theory has hardly been developed at all in the West, and is quite unknown in the English-language literature. There is literature in German, Dutch and Italian (e.g. Schoenfeld, 1974) which considers this aspect of accounting, but since it is theory

137

deduced from the basic axioms of managerial economics, it has little relevance to Islam, for the reasons set out in Chapter 5.

Even those texts which describe the practice of Western managerial accounting have been subject to criticism for a failure to capture what modern industry truly requires by way of managerial information (Kaplan 1983, 1984; Johnson and Kaplan, 1987). It seems as if the traditional techniques of accounting itself are unable to carry the messages needed to plan and control business activity. This is because both financial accounting and managerial *accounting* are aimed at a population of diverse, unknown users, with an unlimited capacity for processing information and an aggressive attachment to the economizing spirit. We have argued that these financial statements comprise two very different elements: an 'events' approach providing information for rational market-making in the company's securities, and a 'valuation' approach which forms part of the rituals dealing with the distribution of surpluses within the enterprise.

By contrast, managerial concerns usually relate to known users, whose capacity for information processing is severely limited by the pressures of business, if nothing else. Above all, they are in real contact with the problems of the company, and therefore likely to be seeking 'common-sense' solutions rather than further abstract analyses. In general, this is achieved through more immediate rituals than the presentation and analysis of accounting information. It is more useful to see such needs as being met by a 'management information system' which carries both financial and non-financial information at a very low level of aggregation. The position is well illustrated by Figure 7.1. This figure emphasizes the fact that while the three alternative assumptions reflect general positions on a continuum with respect to 'Capacity of Human for Information Processing' and the 'Model of Human Decision Making', financial accounting makes no provision for any users apart from a totally diverse and unknowable body of *rentiers*. Managerial accounting assumes that its audience is internal to the company, but is still too diverse for its specific needs to be known. By contrast, a management information system must be able to supply neither more nor less than the precise needs of each individual decision-maker.

By tradition, 'management information systems' are associated with the use of very large, integrated data-bases, maintained on mainframe computers. This does not make the concept invalid as a foundation for a general theory applicable to every kind of business, if only because the continuing enhancement of much smaller computers brings the possibility of using computerized systems within the reach of quite small enterprises. Moreover, any information which is recorded outside the human brain has

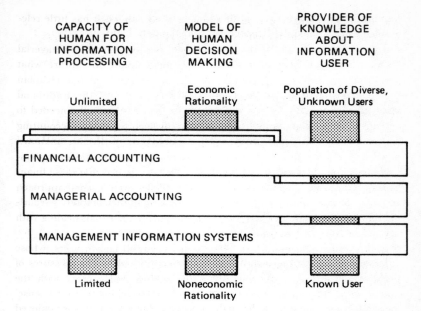

Figure 7.1 *Fundamental assumptions affecting orientations toward information systems.*
Source: Davis (1985, p. 251) reproduced by permission of the publishers.

to be stored 'systematically' if it is to be used at all. It will be remembered (from Chapter 1) that the human brain's capacity for holistic recall is not readily replicated by the computer. Certainly, most definitions of the term 'management information system' emphasize the provision of useful information for specific purposes, without reference to the benefits of consistency of information, which might follow from using a common data-base, e.g.:

> A management information system is an organized set of processes that provides information to managers to support the operations and decision making within an organization. (Kroeber, 1982, p. 9).

The proposition that the same terms should have the same meanings and values every time and in every place where they are used has more validity in financial accounting than in other aspects of the use of externally stored information. In the former case, the emphasis is on economic rationality and an unknown diversity of users. In the latter case, the question is one of supporting the idiosyncratic needs of known users, in decisions where the problems are commonly ill-structured and the data highly uncertain. The objective is to reinforce the manager's innate common sense, as he or she deconstructs some formal, conscious (and subtly incorrect) model of the problem.

This information cannot be common sense *per se*, because it is formally recorded, but it serves as an *aide-mémoire* to the decision-maker's central nervous system. This type of information is a part of the informal information system which exists inside every organization, whether it is a designated part of the 'official' information system or otherwise. Organizations commonly contain a number of unofficial information systems ('little black books', 'grapevines') which supplement the official system. Some of these actually contain material ('counter-information') that is contradictory to the official information. There may be certain sorts of information which need to be known, but which it is not thought convenient to hold on the official record (Gambling, 1984, Chapter 2).

Islam does not recognize a dichotomy between the economic aspects of a problem and any other considerations surrounding it. It follows that the management information system approach is more in sympathy with the ideals of Islam than that of the traditional accounting system. The Muslim proprietor/manager must give the same weight to moral, social and scientific considerations as to purely financial ones. Also, the proposition that information emerges from a dynamic process, as opposed to a static collection of recorded 'facts', emphasizes the need for personal attention to one's affairs at all times.

Moreover, we will argue that Muslims' total commitment to justice might lead them to prefer to place on formal record many pieces of information that would otherwise be a matter of informal record, if they were to be recorded at all. At the same time, it might be expected that 'counter-information' should not exist within the Islamic firm. It cannot be inconvenient for anything that is morally right to be on the official record. What is not morally right ought not to be tolerated. There is no place for unofficial information systems of any kind under Islam. *Shura* (consultation) is a two-way process enjoined upon all Muslims: it follows that Muslim employees have a duty to keep their employers fully informed about matters known to them.

There are good historical reasons why accounting records have been so large a part of the traditional official information system. However desirable, the *ad hoc* assembly of a wide variety of disparate pieces of data is not an easy thing to achieve by clerical methods. Before the invention of the computer, the most economical procedure was to aggregate the basic data into permanent sub-assemblies at a fairly high level of generality. As Figure 7.1 illustrates, financial accounting is well suited to highly non-specific use. Also, the technique of double-entry bookkeeping provides at least a superficial demonstration of the completeness and accuracy of accounting information. The maintenance of a low level of aggregation, and concern for dynamic updating of the data, means that considerable care has to be taken to secure the integrity of the data-base. Especially where the system is a manual one, it would be essential to keep the formal data-gathering to a minimum consistent with the information needs of those who use the system.

A Taxonomy of the Islamic Information System

Much of the content of an Islamic management information system will be comparable with that of its Western counterparts. However, particular concerns of the Shari'a suggest a taxonomy for such a system, which also includes a number of items which might not be of much interest to Western managers, or stockholders:

A. *Justice* (Adalah)

Islam places great emphasis on plain dealing. There is also a specific direction to make a proper record of all contracts, and ensure that their terms are certain, and unambiguous. It follows that a Muslim management would tend to look at matters of contract as an issue in its own right, and not merely as a vehicle for the transactions which occur under them. Moreover, as we have seen, an Islamic company is likely to have an elaborate network of contractual relationships. The information system might be expected to provide information of this type:

1. The full text of all contracts to which the enterprise is a party. Verbal agreements would need to be 'confirmed in writing'.
2. Contracts of service require the payment of fair wages, so the system might be expected to supply, as a routine, the supporting calculation of the 'fair wage' of every person with a contract of service. In an Islamic company, this includes the stockholders and those who supply Islamic loan capital; as with other proprietors, their 'wages' can be extinguished by losses, but the amounts need to be known in order to compute the fair prices of the firm's goods and services.
3. In the same way, the information system should contain the remaining data

needed to compute the fair prices and, indeed, show the calculations supporting all prices charged by the firm.

4. Islam also places emphasis on 'fair trading', so bribery, cartels and all devices aimed at securing unfair advantages in business are strictly forbidden. It is not easy to provide 'negative information', and arrangements of this type are commonly made in secret. Nevertheless, it would be appropriate for an Islamic management to devise a system of internal check and control aimed at making such arrangements very difficult to set up, or execute. The information system should provide evidence that the checks and controls were being operated.

B. *Pursuit of Growth* (Tazkiyah)

Since the pursuit of wealth is actively encouraged by Islam, a Muslim company might be expected to keep a formal record of its ongoing search for the best employment of the funds and talents at its disposal, as well as the plans and budgets which emerge from it. Specific information might include:

1. *Opportunities for development.* Managers might want to know which journals and abstracting services were being read by the responsible staff; progress on research and development projects; the results of suggestion schemes; the activities of competitors.

2. *Long-range plans and policies.* As we have argued in Chapter 6, Islamic managers may be less disposed to quantify such plans at an early date than would be the case with their Western counterparts.

3. and 4. *Budgets and performance against budgets.* These would resemble their Western counterparts, except that they might cover shorter time periods.

5. *Risk management.* For the reasons discussed in Chapter 6, Muslim managers might be expected to pay considerable attention to the risks involved in their decisions. They might be expected to list the Bayesian and statistical probabilities relative to their decisions, and the more or less formal sensitivity analyses underlying them.

C. *Proper Distribution of Wealth* (Zakah)

The valuation of that part of the proprietor's wealth tied up in the enterprise, and its liability to *zakah* taxation, is a central purpose of the Islamic accounting system (Chapter 5), as is the amount of the distributable income. Specific issues might include:

1. Valuations of the assets subject to *zakah*; these would be valued at current market price, possibly using Chambers' CoCoA principles.

2. The control of working capital is essential to the proper calculation of the *zakah*. Questions over the recoverability of debt, and the settlements arrived at with insolvent debtors, will be of greater interest than might always be the case in Western companies.

3. Although Islamic profit calculations will take account of (CoCoA) holding gains and losses, distributable income is based on cash-flow, adjusted for capital maintenance (see D below). The data necessary to make these calculations, and the calculations themselves, should be on record.

4. As was said in Chapter 6, the decision over the exact amount of the dividend to be paid involves important issues of justice and stewardship. An Islamic company might be expected to minute its deliberations on this point in some detail. In particular, care should be taken over the matter of any super-profits, beyond the 'fair remuneration' of the proprietors. Although it is a matter of merit to earn them justly, it may not be appropriate to distribute them, except in exceptional circumstances.

5. *Solvency.* Islam pays especial heed to questions of insolvency; no merit attaches to giving alms, for example, while creditors remain unpaid. It follows that the term is always interpreted in its strictest sense: the ability to pay one's debts as they fall due. Islamic cash-budgets are required to clear outstanding creditors at all times, while taking a suitably conservative view of the possibilities of collections from debtors.

D. *Responsible Shareholding* (Khilafa)

The unique contribution of Islam to modern business practice is likely to be the concept of responsible shareholder behaviour. For the most part, this consists in a personal involvement in the correct management of the enterprise, along the lines described throughout the latter part of this book. However, there are a number of issues relating to capital management which might be a matter of record in the company's information system:

1. *Maintenance of capital.* In a general way, it seems that a firm's capital should only be reduced by trading losses, or by a deliberate repayment of capital, if the firm's undertaking is deliberately being reduced in size. Otherwise, there is a general duty to maintain the undertaking in the very best physical (and spiritual) condition.

2. *Capital erosion.* Something was said of the Islamic position on 'accounting for inflation' in Chapter 5 and its first appendix. We have argued that the necessarily medium-range, managerial approach of Muslim proprietors/managers, and the

usual bases for Islamic taxation, make this a non-issue in Islam. Muslims have a station in life, and they are expected to earn enough to maintain *that*. This is only possible if they maintain an adequate income in the future, which requires appropriate investments to be made in plant and inventories. However, their concern is with what it costs to put in hand whatever needs to be done in the current budget period. 'A fair price' for the company's current output is one which covers these costs, net of the CoCoA valuation of the assets acquired. Hypothetical calculations of 'true economic profit', based upon untestable assumptions about the future, are not part of the Muslim philosophy.

3. *Capital appraisals.* Chapter 6 has suggested that Muslims are not likely to employ the traditional Western discounted cash-flow approach to capital project appraisal. This means that the case for investment will be argued on technological or demographic grounds alone. Clearly, the information system should minute the discussions of these matters, and supply and record whatever supporting (or contrary) evidence existed when the decision to invest was taken.

4. *Business expansion.* The expansion of an Islamic business must be undertaken with due regard to the physical possibility of keeping properly informed of what is happening, and remaining assessible for consultation. Authority cannot be totally delegated. Information would be required about spans of authority, dispersal of units and so on. It will be recalled that this does not necessarily restrict the overall size of an Islamic company; interlocking subsidiaries and the use of franchising will enable such companies to enjoy the economies of scale without detracting from the members' ability to maintain personal contact with those parts of its affairs for which they are responsible. Since Islamic loans are also commonly in the form of a temporary partnership agreement, an Islamic company of any size is likely to be finely segmented in various ways. This complex *corporate* structure replaces the complex *financial* structure of the Western company.

5. *Transfer pricing.* Given this complicated corporate structure, and the requirement for fair pricing and fair trading, it is obvious that an Islamic company needs to pay especial attention to justifying the prices at which goods and services pass between the semi-independent segments of the enterprise. Where arm's-length market prices cannot be found, it may be that the problems traditionally associated with the division of the overall profit do not arise under Islam. *All* prices have to be fair, whether they apply internally or externally. Therefore the transfer prices have to cover the fair remuneration of the managers and investors who are running the segment. The problem, if any, lies with the data contained in A(1 and 3) and in D(4): Is the overall remuneration received by national or international linking managers and shareholders really 'fair'? Can they really hope to pay proper attention to all the segments allegedly under their control?

E. *Interpersonal Relationships* (Shura)

Islam attaches great importance to consultation between proprietors and those affected by their decisions, and the proper succession to offices of all kinds. Accordingly, a Muslim management information system could be expected to contain a good deal of information on personnel matters:

1. *Staff development, appraisal and promotion procedures.*
2. *Suggestion schemes and grievance procedures.* It should be remembered that, in an Islamic company, consultative procedures should apply to all collaborators, including neighbours, suppliers, customers—and even the shareholders themselves.
3. *Share transfer matters.* As we explained in Chapter 4, and its appendix, the shares in Islamic companies cannot enjoy the totally free transferability of their Western counterparts. Even if the other shareholders and managers cannot refuse to register a transfer, it may be that they have a right to prior knowledge of the sale, and an opportunity of discussing the matter with the vending member. There is also the question of the identity of the purchaser; at the least, it may be that he or she should be known under their true name, and be of the Muslim faith. Moreover, all dealings are (in a sense) 'insider trading'. It follows that the Register of Members should contain a considerable amount of information about the circumstances surrounding transfers, including the prices paid for the securities.
4. *Credit policy.* Given the Muslim attitude to insolvency, the granting and seeking of credit is a very serious matter for the Islamic company. There would be particular concern about the adequacy of the credit investigations undertaken. Other matters would be the existing and proposed lines of credit, and the terms of the various compositions which every company can expect to have made with insolvent debtors.

F. National Economic-Planning Statistics

Chapter 3 has described the proactive role of the Islamic State in economic matters. Stable currencies and stable, efficient markets of all kinds are necessary conditions for an Islamic society, as is the virtual absence of criminal activity. It is the principal purpose of an Islamic State to ensure their existence. It follows that the State will require extensive dialogue on such matters, especially with firms that can be considered market-makers, rather than price-takers. Economic statistics prepared for external consumption will make up a large part of the formal, regular output from a Muslim management information system.

The Disclosure of Islamic Corporate Information

As for the disclosure of the data-base, it is obvious that the shareholder/proprietor/manager should have free access to everything it contains. This is the group which 'runs the business'; every member is expected to exercise informed judgement about all major issues affecting the company. One might expect there to be a regular circulation of major changes occurring in Sections A to E, with occasional, more extensive summaries of the entire content.

Sections B, C and D contain the 'market-sensitive information' which has to made available to the Stock Exchange. This includes whatever 'financial statements' may be appropriate for the Islamic company. The essential difficulty has been dealt with at length in Chapter 4: existing shareholders are all 'insiders', so it impossible to place prospective purchasers on the same footing. At the same time, there is little point in attempting to provide them with the level of 'financial accounting' information given to Western investors, since if they do purchase the shares, they will thereby become insiders, with all the duties and liabilities that may involve. The fact is, the market in Islamic shares is likely to be very 'thin' by Western standards. Instead of buying the equivalent of 'common stock in General Motors', one would buy 'common stock in General Motors (Framingham Plant)' and so on. Stockbrokers on such exchanges would probably be rather smaller than their Western counterparts, and tend to specialize in a few classes of security. They would act more like business-brokers, by putting prospective buyers in touch with prospective sellers of shares. Buyers, in particular, would need extensive professional advice before entering into the ownership of shares in an Islamic company.

The factual material in Sections B, C and D should be available to the market specialists, financial journalists, and indeed anyone who expresses an interest in the company. However, the sections do contain other material which could properly be considered confidential to the existing shareholders/managers. This relates to strategies and tactics which are merely under discussion, or have not yet been put into operation. It is right that companies should retain an element of surprise in dealings with their competitors. This is the 'grey area' referred to in Chapter 4; existing members should be aware of these matters, but they need to be careful not to take advantage of a purchaser's ignorance of what is planned. The basic problem of 'insider trading' is the difficulty of guessing what the market reactions to a given piece of information might be. It may be that the problem would be less acute in dealings in the shares of Islamic companies, if only because prospective purchasers would be aware that their vendors must be in possession of some such information, and discount the shares accordingly.

The audit of the material in an Islamic management information system needs some discussion. The material disclosed to the stock market should be subject to a commercial audit in the ordinary way. Compliance with the Shari'a principles will not be a *direct* concern of these auditors, who will merely look for compliance with the appropriate secular legislation. Of course, the secular law in an Islamic State should reflect the relevant Shari'a principles. However, as we have mentioned in Chapter 3, it is often possible to comply with the letter of the law, while contravening its spirit. That is the reason why an Islamic company would place on record the material about contracts and consultation contained in Sections A and E of the taxonomy described above. It may be that these sections would be the subject of a specifically 'religious' audit, of an internal or external nature. The audit would require the professional skill of the *ulama*; possible examples exist in the old office of *hisbah* described in Chapter 3, or in the present-day Religious Advisory Boards of many Islamic banks.

Bibliography

Davis, G. B., 'Different Orientations toward Information Systems', *in* D. L. Jensen, (Ed.), *Information Systems in Accounting Education* (Columbus, Ohio: Ohio State University, 1985), pp. 249–53.

Gambling, Trevor, *Positive Accounting: Problems and Solutions* (London: Macmillan, 1984).

——, 'Accounting for Rituals', *Accounting, Organizations and Society*, Vol. 12 (1987), pp. 319–29.

Johnson, H. T., and R. S. Kaplan, *Relevance Lost: The Rise and Fall of Management Accounting* (Cambridge, Mass.: Harvard Business School Press, 1987).

Kaplan, R. S., 'Measuring Manufacturing Performance: A New Challenge for Managerial Accounting Research', *The Accounting Review*, Vol. LVIII (1983), pp. 686–705.

——, 'The Evolution of Management Accounting', *The Accounting Review*, Vol. LIX (1984), pp. 390–418.

Kroeber, D. W., *Management Information Systems: A Handbook for Modern Managers* (New York: The Free Press, 1982).

Schoenfeld, Hanns-Martin W., *Cost Terminology and Cost Theory: A Study of Its Development and Present State in Central Europe* (Urbana-Champaign, Ill.: Center for International Education and Research in Accounting, 1974).

Epilogue

As we observed in the Introduction to this book, our objective in writing it is not specifically 'religious'. Its intended readers are business people and accountants, both Muslim and non-Muslim alike. For Muslims, we have suggested some new theory which may be of use in the ongoing debate about the organization and management of businesses in an Islamic State. It is sometimes claimed that too little detailed thought is being given to the mechanics involved in setting up such institutions (Naipaul, 1981). The same theory is being offered to non-Muslims, as an alternative vantage-point from which to view their own theories, institutions and methods.

Certainly, we have no thought of converting anybody from one belief to another, or even of promoting a better ecumenical understanding where Muslims and non-Muslims meet in business. One author is a Muslim; for him, the Shari'a is God's revealed Law, and Mohammed is the Seal of the Prophets. His co-author is not a Muslim, and may be supposed to take a contrary view of both of those propositions. Since the book opened with a forthright statement of the Muslim position, it may be just to allow the non-Muslim member of the authorship to close it. Belief in Christianity should not invalidate any virtues which can be seen to exist in the *business* principles which the Prophet expounded. Indeed, speaking as 'the Devil's advocate', it would seem reasonable that, since Mohammed had extensive experience of the business methods of his time, he might be expected to say something of value, in a human capacity, about that aspect of life.

It is unlikely that a non-Muslim would disagree with the propositions that all continuing relationships in a modern human organization must be based upon *khilafa, adalah, shura* and *bay'a*, as defined in these pages. In these less deferential times, attempts to exploit the labour of others without observing these principles will always be seen as open coercion, or a covert confidence trick. In neither case can the relationships survive indefinitely.

148

Moreover, *shura* (consultation) must be a two-way street, and employees, neighbours, suppliers and customers do not merely have a right to exercise *shura*, but a positive duty to exercise what skill and knowledge they possess in advising the capitalist what to do. It is always the latter's sole responsibility to decide whether or not to take the advice, but this has no effect on the duty to offer it.

This philosophy would go beyond employee consultation. Presumably, an Islamic customer ought not to buy from another supplier simply because he or she offers better goods or better terms. First, there is a duty to advise the existing supplier that something is amiss. We now know that this type of approach is not especially other-worldly. Chapter 1 suggested that there is much more to relationships between customer and supplier than the passing of orders, goods and cash. We also know (from Chapter 6 and elsewhere) that the preservation of such relationships is central to modern 'world-class manufacturing' methods.

In conclusion, we believe that the non-Muslim reader will have learned something of value from these pages, irrespective of the religious claims of Islam itself. For whatever reason, the Qur'anic principles which apply to business seem universally sound. The problems encountered in Western organization theory, finance, and accounting theory appear to proceed from a tendency to establish human relationships which are somehow deficient in terms of those principles. People seek advantage from behaving toward the others whom they encounter in business, without full exercise of trusteeship, justice, consultation and loyalty. They actually set up their organizations with structures which limit the operation of these basic principles of 'common-sense' human behaviour.

Those who behave in this way must be unaware that such an approach contravenes what can be perceived of the way in which the Universe operates, quite apart from any considerations of revealed religion, or even humanistic morality. It is to act as if the instinct-reduced models of human perceptions were adequate representations of reality, while denying the full play of common-sense deconstruction which is our only guarantee of long-term survival in the Universe. As for the long search for 'generally accepted accounting principles' described in Chapter 5, it will always be difficult to provide an unambiguous account of ambiguous transactions, carried out by an entity whose structure was intended to promote ambiguity!

Bibliography

Naipaul, V. S., *Among the Believers* (New York: Knopf, 1981).

149

Index